Praise for *China Goes West*

"A thorough and thoughtful examination of one of the most important trends that will help shape the future of business, technology and society. Joel has written a clear account of the globalization journey, helping readers understand the challenges, opportunities, risks and rewards of 'going global'."
  – Yang Yuanqing, Chairman and CEO, Lenovo Group

"Smart, practical and highly readable … In *China Goes West*, Joel Backaler brings an important, accelerating global business trend into timely focus."
  – Mark Duval, President, American Chamber of Commerce in China

"Joel Backaler's book is a real eye-opener. Written in a clear, precise, and ready-to-use manner, it tells the tale of contemporary China's 'Journey to the West'."
  – Davide Cucino, President, European Union Chamber of Commerce in China

"In *China Goes West*, Joel Backaler separates the facts about China's global investment strategy from fiction and fear. Presented as a 'how to' account, Backaler does an exceptional job dissecting a complex topic into clear, easy-to-understand segments about the important economic, political, and cultural aspects of China's expansion. A must-read book for business leaders, MBA students, policy-makers and anyone seeking insight into the global business trend of the century."
  – Steve Burrows, Former CEO, Anheuser-Busch International Inc.

"Joel Backaler's *China Goes West* is a true must-read for business leaders, researchers, and anyone interested in China's rapid economic growth. Backaler details numerous real life business examples and unlocks key cultural and governmental differences in a style that is both refreshing and engaging."
  – Ken Newell, President, PepsiCo Greater China (2008–2012)

"*China Goes West* offers a balanced, readable assessment about one of the key new developments in the global economy – the dynamic, evolving story of Chinese companies' investments overseas. Joel Backaler's book offers pragmatic recommendations for companies and governments looking to engage intelligently in this process. Readers will finish this book with a clear understanding of both the challenges and opportunities this new phenomenon is bringing."
  – Kerry Brown, Executive Director, China Studies Centre, University of Sydney

"Joel Backaler's comprehensive *China Goes West* will be the go-to-guide for those looking to get up to speed quickly on the greatest business story of our time."
  – Julian Chang, Executive Dean, Harvard Kennedy School

"In *China Goes West*, Joel Backaler gives a concise and highly informative overview of Chinese companies' experiences abroad and in their home market. The book is an invaluable introduction to a critical emerging global trend and is both a useful and stimulating reference."
  – Vincent Chang, Executive Dean, Peking University HSBC Business School

"Joel Backaler's fast-paced, accessible book on China's push to invest around the world is destined to become a major resource for anyone wanting to understand and benefit from the rise of global Chinese companies. From city managers looking for investments, to CEO's looking for global partners, to average workers worried about their future, Backaler's book provides a balanced view of the newest chapter in China's rise."
  – John Pomfret, Author of *Chinese Lessons: Five Classmates and the Story of the New China*

China Goes West

Everything You Need to Know About
Chinese Companies Going Global

Joel Backaler

First published 2014 by
PALGRAVE MACMILLAN

Palgrave Macmillan in the UK is an imprint of Macmillan Publishers Limited, registered in England, company number 785998, of Houndmills, Basingstoke, Hampshire RG21 6XS.

Palgrave Macmillan in the US is a division of St Martin's Press LLC, 175 Fifth Avenue, New York, NY 10010.

Palgrave Macmillan is the global academic imprint of the above companies and has companies and representatives throughout the world.

Palgrave® and Macmillan® are registered trademarks in the United States, the United Kingdom, Europe and other countries.

UK ISBN 978–1–137–29392–3
US ISBN 978–1–137–41012–2

This book is printed on paper suitable for recycling and made from fully managed and sustained forest sources. Logging, pulping and manufacturing processes are expected to conform to the environmental regulations of the country of origin.

A catalogue record for this book is available from the British Library.

A catalog record for this book is available from the Library of Congress.

Typeset by MPS Limited, Chennai, India.

Printed in the United States of America

*This book is dedicated to my partner in all aspects of life –
my wife Qian.
Without your unfaltering support, love, and encouragement,
this would not have been possible.
Thank you.*

Contents

List of Figures and Tables

Figures

Tables

Foreword

In 1982, when I first traveled to China, there were few books on doing business in China – or on the Chinese economy for that matter. The market reforms initiated by Chinese leader Deng Xiaoping had only begun four years prior, and the early beginnings of China's economic miracle had yet to catch the attention of the West. That summer, I traveled by train from Heidelberg, Germany, across Europe to Moscow. From there we boarded the Trans-Siberian Railway traveling six days covering 9,000 kilometers (5,600 miles) through the Soviet Union and Mongolia, crossing the Chinese border into the remote town of Erlian. Despite the long train rides, my friends and I spent three of the most fascinating months of our lives touring the vast country from Luoyang in Henan to Emeishan in Sichuan. When we arrived back in Germany, I began searching for ways to return to China to begin my career in what would become the most exciting place on earth to do business.

After moving two years later with my family to Taiwan to study Chinese, I finally had my chance in 1987 to work in mainland China for ABB, a large Swiss engineering conglomerate. At that time, little had changed from my first trip to China. There were no skyscrapers and it seemed as though the tallest building in any given city was no more than six stories high. It was not until 1992 when Deng Xiaoping traveled through the southern provinces of China and delivered his famous message that "getting rich is glorious" that visible signs of China's economic transformation began to appear.

In 1996, I took my second assignment working for a Western multinational in China. I joined BASF, the world's largest chemical company, to serve as its General Manager for China. I spent the remainder of the 1990s simultaneously negotiating four multi-billion dollar projects in Shanghai, Nanjing, and the southern island province of Hainan. Through the support of the visionary BASF CEO Jürgen Strube and the energetic board member Jürgen Hambrecht, we built the foundation for a successful China operation in the midst of the Asian Financial Crisis and despite the complexities of the Chinese approval process. There was a constant need to reassure BASF stakeholders in Germany that the team was making the right decision investing so much in China at this early stage. The vast majority of Western multinationals at that time still divided their geographic operations as Europe, North America, and "Rest of World".

By the early 2000s, the West's attention finally shifted to China. After two decades of sustained economic growth averaging around 10 percent, China's economic progress was hard to ignore. Skyscrapers popped up across first tier cities in Beijing, Shanghai, Guangzhou, and in smaller cities across China. Companies from Europe and the United States began investing millions of dollars in the Chinese market. These firms did not always care about profitability – their mandate from headquarters was to "grow at all costs" and prepare to sell to China's coveted 1.3 billion consumers.

At the same time, my position at BASF required me to travel frequently between my base in China to our headquarters in Germany. It was through this regular back-and-forth travel that a new aspect of China's rise caught my attention. In 2006, I witnessed one of our Chinese competitors, China National BlueStar Group, acquire a large business unit of France's Rhodia and all of Adisseo Group. We had grown accustomed to competing with Chinese firms within China, but this was a completely new phenomenon that was hard to ignore. Since China's "Going Out Policy" was first announced as a result of the 10th 5-year plan, there has been a steady increase in Chinese overseas investment starting around 2000. But around the time of BlueStar's investments in France, there was a big spike that continues to grow tremendously each year.

In 2013, the European Union Chamber of Commerce in China, which I chaired for many years, released a detailed study on Chinese enterprises that have entered and operate in Europe. The Chamber conducted this survey because Chinese investment in Europe has reached over $65 billion since the mid-2000s, with $12.6 billion invested in 2012 alone. The percentage of outbound direct investment (ODI) from China is relatively small given the country's status as the largest contributor to global growth. However, Chinese ODI in developed economies is growing at double digits each year. What began as a state-sponsored push to secure natural resources in developing markets and get capital out of China during the early 2000s has diversified across industries and geographies – especially in the West.

Today, a search for "China business" on Amazon.com yields nearly 60,000 book results, a shocking number considering there were almost none when I first traveled to China more than 30 years ago. The vast majority of these books focus on how to succeed conducting business within China. Yet very few attempt to look at the latest chapter in China's global rise, which is how to do business with China in the global business economy. Even fewer look beyond the initial stage of Chinese outbound investment in developing markets in Asia, Africa, and Latin America to highlight the next phase of investment in advanced economies that will mark an even more dramatic shift from the traditional arrangements of international business. This is why Joel Backaler's book is so important.

His book sheds light on the critical lessons learned by Chinese companies entering markets in the West. He is an excellent storyteller, and uses rich narrative about the executives and officials behind the emergence of this phenomenon to help provide readers with insight into the motivations behind this trend. The book also provides frameworks to understand the key considerations about their rise as well as practical recommendations for how Chinese investment in the West can be mutually beneficial across political, economic, and social realms. Joel Backaler masterfully takes a complex subject of prime importance for anyone in the global business community, and breaks it down into a readily consumable and enjoyable book that informs readers about the next key global business trend to watch.

Joerg Wuttke,
Chief Representative, BASF China,
Former President European Union Chamber of Commerce in China

Acknowledgments

To be able to write this book and dedicate the necessary time, research, and attention to detail – while working a full-time job – required the tremendous support of a number of incredible individuals. I had well over a few hundred conversations and email exchanges with the people listed below. I will be forever grateful for the perspective each of them shared with me over my time spent writing this book.

I would like to give a special thanks to the senior management team of Frontier Strategy Group, particularly Richard Leggett and Mike Fergerstrom, for their flexibility and commitment. This work would not be nearly as strong without the thoughtful edits and feedback from Wendy Leutert and Ashley Woolheater. The following individuals went above and beyond in their support: Jorge Wuttke, David Wolf, Margaret Wei, Justin Knapp, Tony Nash, and Sophie Meunier.

I wish I could detail how each person below made this book a reality, but the following individuals have my utmost gratitude and appreciation:

Craig Allen, Eric C. Anderson, Greg Anderson, Amy Backaler, Donna Backaler, Gary Backaler, Michael Barbalas, Zachary Barter, Bruno Bensaid, Bill Black, Ed Booty, Aaron Brickman, Kerry Brown, Steve Burrows, Dave Carini, Andrew Carr, Amy Celico, Julian Chang, Vincent Chang, Matthew Clearfield, Nancy Cook, Michael Crain, Davide Cucino, Eleanor Davey-Corrigan, Ted Dean, Tom Doctoroff, Amy Dooling, Mark Duval, Linda Eunson, Yufang Gao, Karl Gerth, Kaiser Kuo, Marc Gearin, Doug Guthrie, Yuan Haiying, Dan Harris, Jeff Herman, Victor Ho, Marika Janis, Eric Jon,

John Kao, Robert Kapp, David Ben Kay, Anna Keville, Elaine Kim, Jonathan Krive, Arthur Kroeber, John Larum, Yuxin Lin, John Ling, Scott Markman, James McGregor, Richard McGregor, Christian Murck, David Murphy, Ken Newell, Pin Ni, Graham Norris, Tamsine O'Riordan, Steve Orlins, Jack Perkowski, David Peng, Michael Pettis, Bill Plummer, Jeremy Peruski, John Pomfret, Ely Ratner, Shaun Rein, David Roman, Daniel Rosen, Bill Russo, Dan Schawbel, Jeff Shafer, Michael Schuman, David Shambaugh, Marie Han Silloway, Charles Skuba, Jon Stewart, Sharon Tang, Tingting Tang, Brion Tingler, Jingmin Wang, Yang Wang, Kate Warach, Ross Warner, Tim Weber, Michael Wessel, Jin Yan, Dezhi Yu, Sabrina Zhang, Na Zhao, Haowei Zhang, and Julia Q. Zhu.

About the Author

Joel Backaler is Director at Frontier Strategy Group, a global advisory firm that supports senior executives in emerging markets, and is a member of the National Committee on United States–China Relations. His work focuses on bridging the gap between Western and Chinese businesses, serving as an intermediary and advisor to executive leaders on both sides.

Following a Fulbright Fellowship in Taiwan and advanced Mandarin study at UC Berkeley's Inter-University Program at Tsinghua University, Backaler began working with Atos Consulting's China state-owned enterprise practice in Beijing. In his position at Atos, he took leadership roles in projects including the restructuring of ChemChina following a round of strategic investment from BlackStone Group. During his subsequent career with Frontier Strategy Group, Backaler was part of the founding team of its Asia Pacific office in Singapore, where he worked with Presidents of Asia Pacific for American and European multinationals including Cisco, Danone, Johnson & Johnson, Adidas, and Estée Lauder.

In 2008, Backaler launched TheChinaObserver.com, an award-winning online platform designed to educate and promote discussion among multinational corporations, governments, and other key stakeholders on the topic of Chinese outbound investment. His writing regularly appears in major international media outlets including BusinessWeek, Forbes, BBC, and Fortune. He has lectured at Princeton University, testified before the U.S.-China Economic and Security Review Commission, and frequently speaks at companies and conferences on the topic of Chinese overseas investment.

Backaler, a fluent Mandarin speaker, has worked and lived in Beijing, Shanghai, Taipei, and Singapore. He currently lives in Washington DC with his wife Qian.

Connect with Joel Backaler on Twitter or LinkedIn to stay up-to-date on the latest movements by Chinese firms overseas.

Twitter: joel.backaler
LinkedIn: http://www.linkedin.com/in/joelbackaler
The China Observer: http://thechinaobserver.com

Introduction

It was only 8:00 a.m. and I could barely distinguish the blue and red BlueStar corporate logo through the dark grey Beijing skies. The towering building was home to just one division of ChemChina's $28 billion dollar global empire. Before walking into BlueStar's headquarters for the first time, I could tell that this was not going to be a typical consulting engagement. In addition to producing specialty chemicals, BlueStar also operates a franchise of over 500 fast-food noodle shops across China called Malan Noodle. BlueStar had just received $600 million in strategic investment from Blackstone, an American private equity firm, and it was my job to work with the BlueStar team to help redesign critical business processes in advance of a planned initial public offering overseas. I entered BlueStar's office fully aware that relying on my Mandarin skills to communicate would be far from the most challenging aspect of this assignment.

BlueStar was one of a growing number of Chinese firms expanding into international markets. Its parent company, ChemChina, had already purchased established firms in developed economies including France, Israel, and Australia. The US and EU's slow recovery from the global financial crisis has undoubtedly expedited the frequency and scale of Chinese companies' investments overseas. But the rise of these firms beyond the walls of the Middle Kingdom was bound to happen due to underlying government and business motivations. Growth in Chinese outbound investment has been tremendous. From barely $2 billion through the 1990s to $20 billion in 2006, this figure skyrocketed to more than $70 billion in 2012. These figures continue to grow substantially each year.

Chinese outbound investment has shifted from natural resource projects in emerging markets in the early 2000s to now also include investment in a diverse range of industries and geographies – especially in the West.[1] Chinese companies now operate in nearly every country around the world and at a tremendous scale. Long-established Western brand names like Volvo, Weetabix, AMC movie theaters, and IBM's ThinkPad all now have Chinese owners. New high-profile Chinese investments in the West make headlines in the *Wall Street Journal* and *Financial Times* each week. Chinese companies are playing a more prominent role in the global economy, and it's time for both sides to take a closer look.

China Goes West is intentionally written to be accessible for a wide range of audiences, providing them with a basic understanding of this highly complex and increasingly important phenomenon. Whether you are a China specialist, an executive at a multinational company, or a general reader, *China Goes West* tells a comprehensive story about the global trend that is reshaping the business world as we know it. To shed light on this phenomenon, the book uses a series of personal stories about the executives behind these Chinese firms as well as broader analytic frameworks.

The book answers the following questions:

- **Who?** Who are Chinese companies? What makes them unique?
- **Why?** Why do Chinese companies want to expand overseas?
- **How?** How are Chinese companies expanding overseas?
- **What?** What are the potential concerns, benefits and recommended responses for all parties?

The book is divided into eight chapters, grouped in four parts:

1. The Foundation;
2. The Approach;
3. The Issues; and
4. The Response.

The first part provides a foundation for readers to understand what makes Chinese firms unique, what the economic and political motivations are for their overseas expansion, and questions whether they are truly ready to expand outside of China.

The second part introduces the approach Chinese firms are adopting to "go West." In particular, the two chapters in this part focus on how Chinese companies are building global brands and acquiring Western companies in order to gain new capabilities and market access.

The third part lays out the issues related to Chinese investment in the West. Chapters 6 and 7 respectively outline the potential concerns and benefits associated with Chinese companies' overseas investments.

The fourth part focuses on the responses recommended for all parties. It includes recommendations for the governments, companies and societies of China and the West about how to improve the current state of Chinese overseas investment. This part argues that for meaningful long-term change to occur, it will take a generation of new leaders on both sides from government, business and society to tackle longstanding misperceptions and increase mutual understanding.

The one question not asked above is **"When?"** When does the West need to be prepared to address the myriad issues associated with Chinese firms operating in their backyards? When must Chinese firms begin to understand how to navigate the complex business environments of advanced economies? The answer is NOW. The foreign direct investment shift is already occurring. But the impact of Chinese companies operating in Western markets extends far beyond the global economy into the political and social realms as well. Its significance will only grow in importance in the coming decades. China is going West. Its firms will irrevocably reshape the global business landscape, and their investments herald both tangible benefits as well as potential concerns. Adopting an appropriate response by all parties is critical to ensure that maximum economic and political benefits are achieved.

Part I

The Foundation

chapter 1

The Chemical Noodle Firm: What Makes Chinese Companies Different?

Ren Jianxin, founder of Chinese chemical firm BlueStar, was not a businessman by trade. Nor was he a famous noodle chef, as his side business might suggest. He began his career, like many CEOs of state-owned enterprises (SOEs) in China, by working for the government. Ren served in an advisory role at the Ministry of Chemical Industries, a government position that would be an ideal job for many Chinese. Government jobs in China are commonly referred to as *tiefanwan* (铁饭碗) or "iron rice bowls" because they offer stable lifetime careers. However, Ren did not wish to pursue a lifelong career in government – he wanted to go into business. In 1984, at the age of 26, with a 10,000 RMB loan and seven business partners, Ren left government. He jumped into the chemical cleaning business and founded BlueStar. Ren built his company's initial reputation and business by cleaning industrial boilers. The work was not glamorous, but over time his firm gained a reputation for its high quality chemical cleaning services.[1]

By the age of 32, only six years after founding BlueStar, Ren took part in his first merger and acquisition (M&A) deal in 1990. By 2012, he was an M&A veteran having purchased 107 domestic firms over the course of his career. Even more impressive were his successful acquisitions of four international businesses in France, Australia, and Israel. Through acquisitions at home and overseas, Ren's initial group of seven partners became a global team of 140,000 BlueStar employees by 2013.[2]

As with many Chinese CEOs, Ren made a personal decision during his career to enter a new market in which BlueStar had absolutely no expertise: noodle making. In 1995, he founded the Malan Noodle Company. In an interview with *McKinsey Quarterly*,[3] Ren explains that his original motivation for establishing the noodle chain was to provide an alternative source of employment for chemical factory workers laid off during the course of China's economic reform. Yet there is something incredibly intriguing and ironic about a noodle chain owned by a chemical firm in a nation awash with news reports about chemically tainted milk supplies and other food safety scandals. According to one of Ren's chemical industry peers: "Ren loves noodles. He's from Lanzhou – all across China there are restaurants selling 'Lanzhou noodles'. Every time you meet the guy he takes you out to eat noodles." Ren's passion for noodles and chemical production is certainly a rare combination.

The English version of Malan Noodle's website portrays the chain's noodle-making process as a large-scale industrialized endeavour, rather than painting an image of home-style, hand-pulled noodles. The website states: "China National BlueStar (Group) Corporation has taken on researching the noodle as a kind of fast food since the 1980s." It goes on to describe how the company hired global research and development talent to achieve great breakthroughs "in the standardization, industrialization and chain operation of Chinese-style catering."[4] Upon reading the full company overview, the website visitor is left envisioning a mass-produced industrial product instead of a restaurant choice for dinner.

Ren's story highlights a number of key questions about the differences between Chinese companies and executive leadership and their counterparts in the West. First, what drives Chinese firms to expand into new markets vastly different from their original areas of expertise? What is a Chinese state-owned enterprise and how does it differ from a private corporation in China? What role does the Chinese government play in influencing the development of Chinese companies within China and their efforts to expand globally? The following sections address these questions and serve as a foundation to understand the main topic of the next chapter: *What factors are driving Chinese companies to go global?*

What makes Chinese firms different?

It is easy to look at established multinational companies such as General Electric or Siemens and then to question the capabilities of their recently arrived Chinese competitors. Chinese companies face the same challenges that Western firms encounter when expanding internationally: understanding overseas legal and regulatory procedures, empowering qualified international managers to lead overseas operations, and striking the right balance between a global strategy and localization at the country level. Yet there are additional elements that make Chinese firms unique. The points of difference explored in this chapter are:

1. *Chinese companies are significantly younger than their peers in the West*
2. *The role of government in Chinese business is more "hands-on"*
3. *Chinese state-owned enterprises present unique challenges*
4. *Chinese business leaders take very different paths to power*
5. *Motivations for Chinese firms to expand into new business areas vary*
6. *The Chinese regulatory environment governing overseas investment is complex*

The key takeaway from this chapter is that Chinese companies are very different from established multinational companies in the West. "Different" should not be interpreted as "suspect" or "malicious." Chinese companies now investing overseas have matured in a domestic business environment unlike that of firms from developed countries in Europe or the United States. As a result, the strategies employed to build their initial profitability in China may not necessarily translate into business success in developed markets. As the following sections address each of these differences, they also explore what challenges Chinese companies will need to overcome as they expand into developed markets and compete with established Western firms.

> "Different" should not be interpreted as "suspect" or "malicious."

Chinese companies are young and learning

The Chinese people take great pride in their nation's thousands of years of history and rightly so. The cultural renaissance of the Tang and Song dynasties during AD 618–907 and AD 960–1279 produced great achievements like the creation of paper, gunpowder, the compass, and the printing press. But despite a long cultural history, the relative brevity of China's modern business history cannot compare to that of developed economies in the West. "Corporate China" is significantly younger than "Corporate America" and "Corporate Europe."

Contemporary Chinese business was only beginning to stir in the early 1980s. After the Chinese Communist Party established the People's Republic of China in 1949, Mao Zedong moved quickly to launch Soviet-style industrialization efforts. By 1956, the government announced that the socialist transformation of China's economy was complete. Between 1966 and 1976, China experienced a lost decade during the Cultural Revolution. Mao sought to regain his preeminent position within the Party leadership by attacking capitalism and traditional Chinese culture. In Chinese cities, state-owned enterprises produced necessary goods and services while providing extensive social welfare services through the *danwei* (单位) or work unit system. But with political struggles taking precedence over production in Chinese factories, the consequences to the country's economic productivity and efficiency were devastating.

In 1978, veteran politician and economic reformer Deng Xiaoping pushed China on a new path towards a market economy by promoting gradual growth of the private sector. Most Chinese companies that make

Table 1.1 Comparison of Chinese vs Western firms by years of experience

Industry	Western company	Founded	Chinese company	Founded
Home Appliances	Electrolux	1910	Haier	1984
Beverages	The Coca Cola Company	1892	Jianlibao	1984
Athletic Apparel	Nike	1964	Li-Ning	1990
Medical Devices	Roche	1896	Mindray	1991
Oil & Gas	Chevron	1879	PetroChina	1999

international headlines today did not even exist until the early 1980s. The above table (Table 1.1) illustrates the relative youth of Chinese firms compared with their Western competitors.

In many industries, Western firms have had decades or even a century more of operating experience compared with their Chinese competitors. In contrast, Chinese firms' rapid growth trajectory means that they are learning how to develop their business while transforming into global industry giants at the same time.

A different role for government in business

The relationship between government and business is one of the most unique elements of so-called "capitalism with Chinese characteristics." Scholarly research has gone into great detail dissecting the different organizational forms of Chinese corporations. In simplest form, Chinese companies can be grouped as belonging to one of the following three categories: state-owned, hybrid, and private. State-owned enterprises are a legacy of China's planned economy in which they played the central role in China's industrialization. Hybrid companies refer to former state-owned enterprises that have been privatized, or seemingly private firms with long histories of close ties to central or provincial governments. Private companies, particularly in the technology and biotechnology space, refer to Chinese firms that are not connected to the government and which operate similarly to most American or European firms.

Each of these three general types of Chinese companies interacts with the government in different ways. State-owned enterprises clearly have a much closer connection with the government; however, even hybrid and private firms depend on the government to do business in China. The story of Haier, a hybrid firm that sells consumer and household electronics, illustrates that many of the large companies making moves into the West often owe much of their early development to government support.

Haier had its beginnings in the port city of Qingdao, best known in the West for its beer exports under the brand name "Tsingtao." In 1984, Zhang Ruimin, a young municipal official, assumed leadership of Qingdao Refrigerator Factory, a failing state-owned factory that had been producing second-rate refrigerators since the 1920s. One of the best-known stories of Zhang's career occurred a year into his role. Zhang received a letter from a customer complaining about the quality of his firm's refrigerators. He and his staff went back to the inventory warehouse to inspect the current stock, and they found that 76 refrigerators had defects. Eager to demonstrate that "good enough" is insufficient when it comes to product quality, Zhang assembled his employees on the factory floor and ordered them to destroy the 76 defective refrigerators with sledgehammers.[5]

In addition to changing the company's culture, Zhang needed to gain access to advanced technology from abroad to improve the competitiveness of the firm's products. In 1986, he forged a partnership with German refrigerator firm, Liebherr Group. The joint venture refrigerators were marketed under the name Qindao-Libohaier (琴岛－利勃海尔). Like many Chinese–foreign joint ventures, Zhang's firm gradually took back complete control of the company once it had access to advanced Western technology. At that point, he took the "Haier" name, using the last two characters of the joint venture brand as its new corporate identity.

As Zhang transformed Haier from a single failing state-owned refrigerator factory into a global household and consumer electronics giant, he relied on the Qingdao government for support. In the late 1980s, when his firm needed new land to expand its manufacturing facilities, the Qingdao government provided Haier with free land in its Yellow Island municipality.

Government officials even went so far as to remove an existing state-owned factory already operating on the island to make room for Haier's expanded operations.[6] Around the same time, the Qingdao government required Haier to assume ownership of Red Star Washing Machine, Derby Freezer, and Light Air Air-Conditioning[7] – three state-owned firms suffering from poor performance. Assigning smaller state-owned firms to be absorbed by larger, better-performing SOEs was a common practice employed by the government during market reforms. While Haier was not an SOE, as a large successful company, the Qingdao government treated it in a similar fashion. Further blurring the line between state and independent ownership, in 2004 Haier became one of the only non-state owned firms to be supervised by Qingdao's State-owned Assets Supervision and Administration Commission, the government body charged with managing state-owned enterprises.[8]

Despite its status as a non-state owned enterprise, support from Qingdao's government was instrumental in building Zhang's firm. Haier has become one of the most successful Chinese companies doing business inside China and overseas. However, it is unlikely to have been so successful without the ongoing mutually beneficial relationship it developed with the Qingdao government.

Government influence in business varies not only by what type of firm is doing business, but also by which city or province in which the company operates. Haier currently positions itself as a collective firm, owned by its employees but, as the previous section explained, the Qingdao government has been by its side throughout the course of its development. It was important for Qingdao to be able to count Haier's business achievements in with those of state-owned firms in its municipality in order to demonstrate high economic performance to the Shandong provincial and Chinese central governments. David Johnson,[9] a 20-year China business veteran, gives an example illustrating the difference between provincial and central government approaches. Johnson was on a management visit to Guangdong province while working for a Western telecommunications firm interested in purchasing a Chinese company there.

He sat down with the Chinese management team to review the due diligence report, and his treasurer asked if anybody had any questions.

Johnson:	"In your financial statements are there any tax rebates from the local government?"
Chinese GM:	"Yes, we received 4–5 different rebates from the local government."
Johnson:	"You wouldn't happen to have any other special government incentives?"
Chinese GM:	"Yes. Last year we expensed over two million dollars worth of capital equipment."
Johnson:	"Why did the local government do this?"
Chinese GM:	"They treat us like a high-tech enterprise, this is their way of encouraging the industry's development."

The Chinese idiom, *tian gao, huangdi yuan* (天高，皇帝远) translates in English to "heaven is high, the emperor is far away." It is often used to describe the situation illustrated by Johnson's story. When the Chinese central government issues guidelines and regulations for doing business in Beijing, provincial governments are often able to operate by a different set of rules because the country's vast size makes central enforcement much more difficult away from the capital. The Chinese firm Johnson met with positioned itself as a private company but, as his questions revealed, it received government support which should not have been offered to a company of its ownership structure and industry. In reality the municipal government offered the firm preferential policies because the firm's high performance was also politically advantageous to it and the provincial government.

Municipal and provincial governments have specific key performance indicators (KPIs) they must meet; similar to how a company might measure the performance of its employees. The local government of Qingdao is no different – which is why its officials were so eager to include Haier's revenues in its regular economic reports to Beijing despite the fact that Haier was not technically a state-owned firm. When a large Chinese firm is successful domestically and globally, municipal and provincial governments benefit from the taxes they collect from the firm. More importantly, their officials benefit from being viewed more favorably by the Chinese Communist Party. Successful local economic performance may lead to career advancement for senior officials and even broader central government support for their province.

> Government influence in business varies not only by what type of firm is doing business, but also by the city or province in which the company operates.

Business leaders running Chinese firms learn from the very beginning of their careers that the government can always promote or hinder their firm's development. This is why Chinese executives are often surprised after their firms expand overseas for the first time to discover that business and government operate much more separately in Western economies. Private Chinese companies, especially in the technology and biotechnology industries, have a less direct relationship with government. Hybrid firms may seek to cultivate close ties to local officials in order to gain access to the preferential policies enjoyed by state-owned companies (SOEs). SOEs are technically owned and managed by the state, making their relationship with government even deeper and often more opaque.

The historical evolution of state-owned enterprises

In the early days of the People's Republic of China, SOEs were central vehicles by which the Party provided necessary goods and services to citizens. At that time, SOEs were just as much political and welfare-providing units as well as economic entities. Business leaders of state-owned firms worked to follow government orders and fulfill their contracts, not make profits. By the early 1990s, new SOE reforms were implemented under Deng Xiaoping and firms began operating on a more commercial basis under the dual-track system of fixed and market prices. At the national level, the Chinese government continues to appoint board members and senior executives to the remaining one hundred or so centrally owned SOEs through the State-owned Asset Supervision and Administration Commission (SASAC). However, in practice state-owned enterprises typically manage day-to-day business activities with limited intervention from the government.

In *The Party*, Richard McGregor describes the evolution of SOEs:

> Once written off as dinosaurs of a crumbling communist system, the structure, solvency and profitability of scores of big state enterprises were transformed in a decade. The giants of communist industry were suddenly throwing off billions of dollars in profits, courtesy of government protection from competition, cheap capital and efficiencies wrenched out of the companies during their overhaul. In 2007, the year which marked the historic high-point of fast economic growth in China, the combined profitability of centrally owned state enterprises reached $140 billion, compared to close to zero a decade before, and triple the earnings of five years before.[10]

Answering to stakeholders, not shareholders

Who are SOE business leaders accountable to? For Western firms, the answer is simple – Western firms are charged with maximizing business value for their shareholders. But in addition to technical business shareholders, Chinese SOEs also answer to political stakeholders in the Party who have a vested interest in the company's success. In *The Party*, McGregor explains the emergence of SOEs that are led by ambitious and commercially driven CEOs, but are managed by the Party behind the scenes. "The corporate animal that emerged from the protracted and painful birth of China Inc. was a strange new beast. Just as the Party had ordered, it was both commercial and communist at the same time."[11] Chinese SOE business leaders are torn between building profitable companies while ensuring their decisions meet the expectations of their Party owners in SASAC.

Protected industries

The next factor that both propels and protects Chinese SOEs is the presence of so-called "strategic industries" in the Chinese economy. There are currently 18 sectors[12] where foreign competition is limited. SOEs are the major players in most of these strategic sectors and therefore the top beneficiaries of these protectionist policies. Table 1.2 lists selected industries closed by the Party to foreign investment.

Access to financing

Typically when companies in the West require financing, firm representatives go to a bank and apply for loans, or they receive capital from a variety of investors in exchange for partial ownership in their firm. The situation in China is very different – especially for state-owned versus private firms.

Chinese SOEs benefit from a number of government advantages that support their business. The first and critical advantage is financial support from the government – in the form of preferential loans from state-owned banks and direct government subsidies. According to Christian Murck,[13] former director of J.P. Morgan China: "The challenge for the continued sustainability of the SOE model is financial support from the Chinese banking system, because they receive privileged access to bank loans." Low interest loans from the government allow SOEs to significantly undercut private competitors and extend favorable credit terms to their customers that would be unrealistic for Chinese or Western private firms

Table 1.2   The 18 strategic industries in China

Automotive	Information Technology	Petrochemicals
Aviation	Insurance	Power
Banking	Machinery	Railways
Coal	Media	Shipping
Construction	Metals	Telecom
Environmental Technology	Oil and Gas	Tobacco

to offer. But lending to SOEs is not always based on rigorous assessments of loan quality, and there are not even strict requirements that SOEs pay back loans at all. From 2011–2012, non-performing loans issued by Chinese state-owned banks to SOEs are estimated to have increased by $10.4 billion.[14]

According to a 2011 study conducted by Unirule, an independent Chinese policy research center, the majority of SOEs are not profitable once you dig into the numbers. The study found that from 2001 to 2008, SOEs did not make any real profits after accounting for low-cost land use, financing and other resources provided by the government.[15] Under the current system, SOEs do not need to be profitable to grow domestically or even internationally. The state is willing to continue its preferential financial policies toward SOEs because it wishes them to serve political and strategic as well as economic goals.

Unlike state-owned and hybrid enterprises, the majority of private firms in China lack the size and influence to obtain financing from state-owned banks. Unable to access official loans, businesses often turn to family, friends – and the informal "shadow banking" sector for capital. Shadow banking refers to any financing provided to a Chinese company by a "non-bank" entity. According to Reuters, China's shadow banking industry is comprised of "thousands of unofficial credit providers, pawn shops, trust firms and various other loan vehicles."[16] The shadow banking sector was allowed to flourish without much government intervention, because private companies helped offset the cost of supporting unprofitable SOEs while Beijing tried to maintain high levels of economic growth. 2013 estimates by global investment bank UBS put the size of the shadow banking system at $3.4 trillion – equivalent to 45 percent of China's GDP.[17] According to analysis by information services and advisory firm Frontier Strategy Group, the shadow banking system has often replaced formal banks in providing finance for private Chinese companies (see Figure 1.1).[18]

The unregulated nature of China's shadow banking sector makes the lending distributed by its institutions inherently more risky than standard

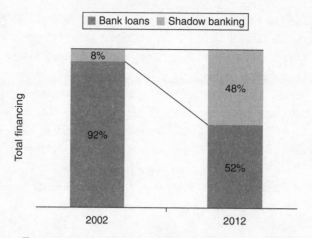

FIGURE 1.1 Shadow banking lending in China (2002 vs 2012)
Source: Q1 2013. *China Quarterly Market Review*. Frontier Strategy Group Analysis.

bank loans. Without visibility into the credit worthiness of its borrowers, shadow-banking lenders are highly exposed to borrower default. Given the major contribution of informal loans to the Chinese economy, the government is working to increase regulation. While this is positive for the Chinese economy's overall stable development, in the short-term this could make it more difficult for private firms to obtain necessary financing to build and operate their businesses at home and overseas. State-owned companies' access to preferential financing provides them with a substantial competitive advantage over Chinese private firms and competitors from international markets alike.

State-owned firms and competition

With their easy access to capital and preferential treatment from the government, state-owned companies make it hard for private enterprises to flourish in certain industries. For example, the airline industry has been and continues to be highly dominated by the state. In 2005, Wuhan-based East Star Airlines was awarded one of the first licenses to operate a private airline company in China. The fledgling airline developed exceptionally quickly. Starting with a single route from Wuhan to Shanghai in 2006, its routes grew to 48 daily flights to cities across mainland China, along with direct routes from Wuhan to Hong Kong and Macao by 2008. Operating an airline requires a tremendous amount of capital for expenses including aircraft leases, fuel, airport services and employee salaries. East Star quickly accumulated 3.8 million RMB (approximately $540,000) of debt and filed for bankruptcy in 2009.[19] At the same time, state-owned China Eastern Airlines was in the process of acquiring Shanghai Airlines despite writing off a 13.9 billion RMB (approximately $2 billion) loss the previous year. SASAC provided China Eastern with 7 billion RMB (approximately $1 billion) to keep the firm afloat.[20] If East Star had been a state-owned airline like China Eastern, it could easily have secured the 3.8 million RMB it needed to keep operating rather than having to file for bankruptcy. Ultimately, East Star's assets were acquired by Chinese state-owned Air China as it sought to expand its flight routes in Wuhan.

While state-owned firms may always have an upper hand competing in those industries deemed strategic by the government, they are not guaranteed the number one spot in other industries. After the success of Chinese internet search firm Baidu (private by this book's definition, but listed publicly on the NASDAQ stock exchange), the Chinese government wanted its own homegrown search engine to better monitor Chinese netizens' searching habits. In September 2010, it launched *Renmin Sousuo*, a state-owned internet search engine. Lacking the right talent, investment, and development strategy, *Renmin Sousuo* or *Jike.com* as it is currently known, never made a dent in China's internet search market. According to Bloomberg, as of 2013 Baidu still dominates the online search industry in China with 80 percent market share.[21]

An evolving SOE landscape

The Chinese government is placing heavy emphasis on SOE reform to level the playing field between state and private sectors. The Party leadership understands that there are unsustainable imbalances between a state sector that is only profitable before accounting for state support and a private sector supported by unregulated shadow banking loans which amount to 45 percent of GDP. At Chinese Premier Li Keqiang's first news conference in March 2013, he publicly committed to allowing private businesses to compete more fairly with state-owned enterprises.[22]

Fundamental questions need to be answered about how independent the government will allow its SOEs to become. While SOEs seek economic and organizational autonomy, the state wants them to serve political as well as economic goals. So which takes priority? As SOEs continue to expand into international markets, the Party will also have to address the issue of accountability. Who will take responsibility for an SOE that makes a bad investment overseas?

However, the effects of ongoing SOE reforms are already emerging. For instance, the number of central state-owned firms managed by SASAC continues to decrease. From 2003 to 2013, the number of central SOEs under its management dropped from 196 to 113.[23] In 2005, China's largest state-owned steel producer, Baosteel, became the first SOE to implement an independent board of directors. By 2012, this number had increased to 50 central SOEs, with 23 of these firms being part of the Fortune 500 including China's three largest oil and gas companies, its two largest telecommunications providers, and the two largest transport and logistics firms.[24]

China observers are well aware that the amount of reform to China's state sector needed to correct the underlying imbalances within the Chinese economy will take time. Even though SOEs might be commercially inefficient at the macro level, they are extremely valuable to certain stakeholders with a vested interest in protecting their favorable position. This class of stakeholders overlaps to a large degree with the political elite and its relatives, which makes reform extremely difficult to implement. In 2012, a stinging *New York Times* exposé of then Prime Minister Wen Jiabao pieced together public corporate records linking 20 of Wen's relatives and friends to assets in excess of $2 billion.[25] Wen Jiabao's family fortune only hints at the deep-rooted political interests that contribute to preventing quicker SOE reforms. For now, the unique nature of SOEs will continue to play a key role in China's globalization efforts.

For now, the unique nature of SOEs will continue to play a key role in China's globalization efforts.

Business leaders take different paths to power

Chinese executives' career paths may vary significantly depending on the type of company they work for. On the one hand, the career path of an executive like Li Yizhong, former Chairman of state-owned oil and gas giant Sinopec, seems to have been shaped heavily by the Chinese government. On the other hand, the story of e-commerce visionary Jack Ma appears strikingly similar to that of a Silicon Valley tech entrepreneur like Steve Jobs or Bill Gates. Their stories (below) shed light on the different paths Chinese executives take to power.

Li Yizhong graduated from Beijing Petroleum University in 1966 and began his career in the petroleum industry as an engineer with Shandong Shengli refinery. He proved himself an astute manager and spent the next 30 years rising through the ranks at Sinopec, one of China's largest state-owned oil and gas firms. As he successively gained more managerial power within Sinopec, Li was awarded Chinese Communist Party (CCP) membership in 1980. With each new role Li assumed, he gained greater access to and involvement with the Party, including appointment to the CCP Central Committee. By the end of his corporate career, Li had run the entire company, first serving as general manager of Sinopec in 1998 and later as chairman of the firm 2000–2003. After his long tenure with Sinopec, Li transitioned to a career in government. Immediately following his role as chairman of Sinopec, Li was appointed deputy director of the State-Owned Assets Supervision and Administrations Commission (SASAC). In 2008, he became secretary of the newly created Ministry of Industry and Information Technology (MIIT), before retiring in 2010.[26]

Li began his career in business as a humble engineer who rose to become CEO of one of China's largest SOEs, and then subsequently held positions of increasing authority in government. *Did Li switch from the business realm to government, or was he working in government from the moment he started working for an SOE?* When dealing with SOEs, the line between the state and corporate sector is extremely blurred. It might seem that Li rose in Sinopec solely through his hard work and management skills. But while he was likely selected early on as a high-potential employee for Sinopec, he was also concurrently tapped as a high-potential contributor to the political and economic goals of the Party. The leaders of Chinese SOEs often prove themselves in business first (like Li) and then transition to government, or they begin in government and then have the opportunity to enter business (as was the case for ChemChina's Ren).

Jack Ma, founder of private e-commerce firm Alibaba Group, took a very different path to corporate power. Ma grew up near Hangzhou, a city south of Shanghai renowned for its beautiful West Lake, *longjing* green tea, and historic temples. The picturesque city has long drawn tourists from across China and around the world. As a boy, Ma was not a particularly good student, but his passion for learning English motivated him to ride his bike to downtown Hangzhou to practice English by speaking with Western tourists, and eventually leading them on tours of the city. After failing his college entrance exam twice, he eventually gained admission to one of Hangzhou's least prestigious universities, and took a job as an English teacher upon graduation.

Ma sat restless in his academic office, a fervent ambition to do international business eating away at him as he graded tests and papers. He began applying for jobs outside of academia, but with no success – he was even turned down for a position as the secretary for a general manager at Kentucky Fried Chicken. In 1995, his luck began to change when his English language skills earned him the opportunity to travel to Seattle as an interpreter for a trade delegation. It was there where he typed in the phrase "China beer" online and did not find any information about the Chinese beer market. China was already fast becoming the world's largest beer market, and Ma was astonished that there was no information about it online.

With no technology background, he returned to China intent on building an online searchable directory to help Chinese businesses connect with the world. His first venture failed, but Ma built a positive reputation in China's nascent internet industry and earned a loyal following of like-minded peers. In 1999, Ma invited 18 fellow entrepreneurs to his apartment for a 2-hour founding speech, inspiring the group to invest together in his business idea and to join as the first team members of Alibaba.com, an online business-to-business trading platform. Ma's relentless focus and ability to effectively articulate his vision and inspire those around him transformed Alibaba Group into the dominant e-commerce player in China. Alibaba Group now continues to expand globally, with Ma having successfully convinced Goldman Sachs, Japan's SoftBank, and Yahoo! to invest millions of dollars in his firm.[27]

Chinese business leaders take vastly different career paths depending on whether they lead state-owned, hybrid, or private firms. An entrepreneurial CEO of a private Chinese firm, like Jack Ma, may follow the more familiar path of famous Western entrepreneurs in their respective industries. However, CEOs of state-owned and many hybrid firms may take a much more directed path, lifted upward through the ranks by the government's hand. However, the leaders of Chinese firms of all types take a very hands-on approach to managing their businesses, especially when it comes to expanding into new products and services.

Chinese companies expand for different reasons

As Western firms grow, they most often look to expand vertically, creating or buying into business areas that complement their core business and give them better pricing and more opportunities to make money in their current industry of focus. Conversely, when Chinese firms grow, they often do so horizontally, expanding into new product or service areas very different from their core business. The result is a series of large conglomerates that are technically focused in one industry; but also have many divisions in other sectors. ChemChina's ownership of Malan Noodle is one example (Figure 1.2).

Another example is Dalian Wanda, the Chinese real estate development firm that purchased AMC Entertainment in the U.S. for $2.6 billion in 2012 and British yacht maker Sunseeker for £320 million (approximately

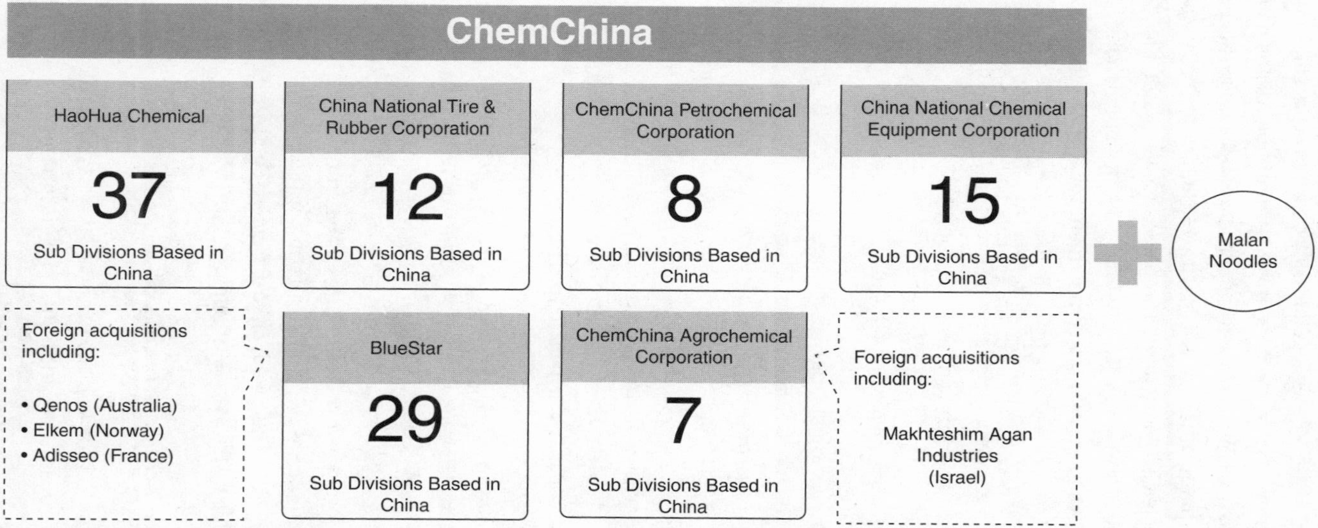

FIGURE 1.2 ChemChina domestic and overseas subsidiaries

Source: **Author's own image, statistics from ChemChina.com.**

$500 million) in 2013.[28] Wanda technically operates across commercial real estate, luxury hotels, movie theaters, movie production, department store chains and even e-commerce. What happens when companies like Wanda go against a competitor that focuses exclusively on one industry like luxury hotels or e-commerce? Most often the company with laser focus on one particular product or service category will have the upper hand, because their other business lines are more complementary.

But Chinese firms "go horizontal" for four main reasons: "uninformed opportunism," "competition-driven diversification," "the *guanxi* effect," and increasingly "market-driven diversification."

Uninformed opportunism

There is often a lack of business discipline in China. Business discipline can be understood as the ability of a company's leadership to make choices that will help develop a business over the long-term, instead of focusing on short-term opportunistic "quick wins" that are not aligned with their overall business strategy. When presented with an opportunity to purchase a company at home or overseas, or to invest in a new area, Chinese business leaders tend to jump quickly, rather than step back to consider whether or not the new opportunity fits with the firm's long-term business strategy. Take the example of Li Tuchun, a former farmer turned dairy drink mogul, who founded Hunan Taizinai in 1996. His firm's flagship product was a special type of yogurt drink that helped promote digestion. At its peak, Hunan Taizinai had over 75 percent of the market for the digestive drink category from 2003 to 2005. However, just when the firm was recording record earnings, Li began to diversify rapidly into new product categories including infant formula, children's clothing, hotels and real estate – all of which lost money. Through Li's uninformed opportunism, Hunan Taizinai went bankrupt in 2010.[29]

Competition-driven diversification

The second reason Chinese firms expand into a variety of business lines is "competition-driven diversification." Mobile phone stores in China are the perfect environments to observe first-hand the level of cut-throat competition among Chinese businesses. Loud music lures shoppers in megamalls filled with retail booths seemingly all selling the same products, while aggressive sales agents shout out their latest "promotions." These are far from the most distracting elements of the shopping experience though. Once Chinese shoppers peer through the glass countertop of a mobile phone sales booth, they are bombarded by the sight of hundreds of brands – well-known international brands like Samsung, LG, and Nokia and lesser-known Chinese brands like Xiaomi, Bubugao (BBK), and Kupai. It is very difficult for consumers to decide on a purchase unless they research ahead of time and know exactly what they are looking for. This intense competition in its core industry is what forces BBK to produce a diverse range of products in addition to mobile phones, including: DVD players, soy milk makers, electronic dictionaries, and rice cookers.[30] Competition is just as fierce in each product category it operates in and the margins it earns are razor thin. Companies like BBK enter multiple disparate business lines because the way they make money is by earning thin margins on a wide variety of products. Together, the total profits are significant enough to sustain its business. Competition pressures Chinese companies to compete primarily on price, offering low prices across different product lines, in order to earn sufficient revenues.

The *guanxi* effect

The third driver explaining why Chinese firms enter multiple business lines may be the most fascinating of them all – and in many cases it has nothing to do with economic factors. Most businesspeople and China experts emphasize the importance of *guanxi* (关 系) when doing business in China. *Guanxi*, which translates as "relationships," is a critical resource for conducting business in any country. Whether you're operating in a business environment governed by contracts or one based on more informal agreements, ultimately people do business with people they like, or at least trust. In China *guanxi* may lead business leaders to make decisions or pursue opportunities that may be entirely unrelated to their original business strategy. The *guanxi* effect helps to explain situations in which a "big boss" or *dalaoban* (大老板) decides to purchase a company or enter a new business line based purely on the recommendation of his or her close confidants.[31]

Market-driven diversification

The last reason why a Chinese firm may choose to enter new product or service categories is the changing dynamics of its operating environment. Chinese executives accustomed to thriving in a Chinese economy growing at annual rates in excess of 10 percent are finding it hard to adjust to the "new normal" of more moderate growth. As a result, demand for products and services in many industries is on the decline and Chinese business leaders need to seek out new areas of expansion. China's industrial sectors were hit hardest following 2008 government stimulus measures to increase capacity for infrastructure projects. As a result of government support, in the forms of loans issued by state-owned banks and subsidies, Chinese firms produced approximately 50 percent of the world's aluminum and steel. Then U.S. Treasury secretary Hank Paulson commented: "When you have administrative measures you get huge overcapacity and [China] has created overcapacity in a whole lot of areas."[32] By June 2013, the China Iron and Steel Association (CISA) reported 86 of China's large and medium-sized steel companies accumulated more than $486 billion in debt leading to a wave of bankruptcies.[33] Overcapacity in the steel industry forced many steel businesses to look into non-steel related businesses to compensate for industry overcapacity.

Baosteel, China's largest state-owned steel producer, has ambitious plans to expand into new business areas. By 2015 the firm plans for non-steel business lines to contribute to nearly half of its annual sales. Wuhan Iron and Steel Corp. announced that it would invest in new areas in agriculture including green farming and pig husbandry. According to CISA, the non-steel business turnover of China's seven largest steelmakers accounted for 23 percent of their total revenues as of 2013.[34] Overcapacity induced by government policy in other industries will certainly lead companies in a range of industries to expand beyond their core product offering to avoid bankruptcy in the coming years.

Chinese companies are regulated differently

The process for Chinese companies to expand internationally is highly convoluted due to the multiple government agencies involved. For large state-owned firms, the process can be much more straightforward because of preferential government treatment and financial support from state-owned banks. However, for emerging private companies in sectors such as the Internet and biotechnology, it is a challenging regulatory puzzle to put together. There are five main government bodies involved in Chinese outbound investment. This book does not provide a step-by-step guide for how different types of Chinese firms interact with relevant government agencies governing outbound investment procedures. However, the following five government agencies are "must knows" for understanding the current byzantine web of government agencies involved in approving overseas investments by Chinese firms going global.

Figure 1.3 gives a bird's-eye overview of the role each government agency plays in facilitating Chinese outbound investment.

i. *National Development and Reform Commission (NDRC)* 国家发展改革委员会
The NDRC plays a central role in China's economic planning. It is the government's chief ministry-level economic planning body, and has

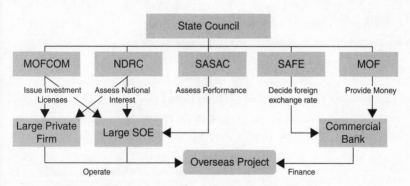

FIGURE 1.3 / **Chinese regulatory bodies for overseas investment**
Source: **Author's own image based on H. Voss (2011), author interviews and analysis.**

authority over outbound investment project approvals and national medium- to long-term economic plans. The NDRC assesses whether the overseas project is aligned with China's national interests. All overseas investment projects are subject to review and approval by the NDRC or its counterparts at the provincial level depending on deal size.[35] The NDRC instituted new measures in 2012 that do not require NDRC approval for "resources development projects" below $300 million or "non-resources projects" under $100 million.[36]

ii. *Ministry of Commerce (MOFCOM)* 商务部
In addition to the NDRC, MOFCOM approval is also necessary for Chinese firms going global. MOFCOM regulates both domestic and foreign trade, works to attract foreign investment, and helps Chinese companies abroad. MOFCOM issues the Overseas Investment Certificate for ratified overseas investment transactions. The certificate serves as the document of record including key investment details such as where the investment will take place, what form of investment it is (greenfield, M&A, equity stake, other), and the deal amount. Chinese companies must obtain an Overseas Investment Certificate from MOFCOM before negotiating with other government agencies such as tax, foreign exchange and customs.[37]

iii. *State-Owned Assets Supervision and Administrative Commission of the State Council (SASAC)* 国务院国有资产监督管理委员会
State-owned firms must also seek approval from SASAC, a state ownership agency that is responsible for managing China's central SOEs – from appointing top executives, to approving mergers and acquisitions, to drafting the laws which govern them.[38] According to Barry Naughton, professor at the University of California, San Diego, "SASAC's mandate is to 'own' these corporations [SOEs] and to manage them in the public interest."[39] Its main objective is to increase the profitability and value of the state-owned enterprises underneath its control. SASAC approval is required for a central SOE to invest overseas.

iv. *State Administration of Foreign Exchange (SAFE)* 国家外汇管理局
SAFE manages China's extensive foreign exchange reserves. Administratively it is located under the People's Bank of China (PBOC), China's central bank.[40] Given that the renminbi is not yet fully convertible

into other currencies, SAFE is a key player in facilitating international transactions to support Chinese firms venturing abroad. In January 2013, SAFE opened a dedicated unit called SAFECo-Financing to further promote Chinese outbound investment. Four months later in May, SAFE also opened an overseas office in New York City.[41]

v. *Ministry of Finance (MOF)* 财政部

The MOF monitors funding for government-related investments. The MOF also approves the writing off of debts and provides money to the state system.[42] *Through injecting capital into state banks, Chinese SOEs are able to gain access to necessary funding for overseas investments.*[43]

Key takeaways from this chapter

Chinese companies are coming from a fundamentally different operating environment from their Western counterparts. The key factors that differentiate the operations of Chinese firms from their peers in the West are their relative youth, their motivations for expansion, how they are managed, and their relationship with government actors. The amount of direct influence the government has over Chinese firms varies depending on whether the firm is state-owned, hybrid, or private, in addition to the overall size of the company itself. The interaction between companies and government also varies significantly depending on the industry and whether interactions are taking place in Beijing or faraway cities and provinces, given the difficulty of policy implementation outside the capital.

The next chapter discusses how the unique characteristics of Chinese businesses impact their leaders' decisions to expand outside of China. Some companies expand into new business lines due to the fierce competition at home, which can make entering overseas markets the best option to maintain growth rates. Other companies seek to align themselves with government policies and to acquire key technologies to boost their firms' competitiveness back home. And still others are motivated by the *guanxi effect* and enter new markets based on the recommendations of their close confidants. Regardless of their motivations, all will face significant challenges due to their relative youth and limited experience in doing business overseas.

chapter 2

Fleeing the Great Game: Why Are Chinese Companies Going Global?

Beginning in the late 1990s, headlines about massive investments in China by Western multinational companies became an everyday occurrence. "Procter & Gamble will invest $1 billion in China," "The Coca-Cola Company plans to invest $4 billion in China over the next three years," and "Cisco is placing a $16 billion bet on the China market" are just a few examples. China was quickly becoming the world's largest recipient of foreign direct investment (FDI) under new reform and opening efforts known collectively as its *qing jinlai* (请进来) "please come in" policy. Chinese firms competed fiercely among themselves and with their new Western competitors to establish themselves as market leaders in their respective industries. At the same time, China adopted a new stance on overseas direct investment (ODI) expressed as *zou chuqu* (走出去) "go out." The "go out" policy, announced in 1999 by the Central Committee of the Chinese Communist Party and formally initiated in October 2000, encourages and supports Chinese companies to invest overseas through incentives and subsidies as well as liberalization of regulatory systems and administrative rules. Chinese government officials commonly use both phrases together[1] when discussing China's development strategy as *qing jinlai, zou chuqu* (请进来,走出去): the government both welcomes foreign companies in to China while encouraging its own firms to "go out."

Why are Chinese companies going global when the domestic market in China seems so vast? Aren't there 1.3 billion customers waiting for the latest and greatest products and services from Chinese firms? To begin, the dynamics of the global business environment have changed dramatically since companies from around the world began to invest in China in record numbers during the 1990s. The days of sustained 10 percent year-on-year growth are over and likely never to return. The cost of labor in China has increased and forced companies to consider producing in other low cost emerging markets in Asia or Africa or even back home. Competition is fierce. In Europe and the US, even long-standing firms have faltered in the wake of the global economic crisis. The M&A market for Chinese buyers in Western economies is ripe as Western companies need capital, citizens need jobs, and governments need tax dollars to help rebuild. These deeper economic shifts have only accelerated the inevitable emergence of Chinese companies on the international stage.

Chinese companies expand abroad due to both government motivations and business necessity. The government wants overseas markets in which to invest its vast foreign exchange reserves, it needs natural resources to sustain China's economic growth, and it can expand its soft power through the development of "national champions" (Chinese firms able to compete globally in key industries). The business case for international expansion is even more straightforward. Chinese firms seek advanced technology, international talent, global brands, and access to new markets. Chinese companies may choose to invest overseas for any one or combination of these factors.

> Chinese companies expand abroad due to both government motivations and business necessity.

A government mandate to "go out"

Ge Li is known as a *haigui* (海龟) or "sea turtle," a term used to refer to Chinese nationals who are educated and gain initial work experience overseas and then return to China. China's economic growth has made it much more attractive for its sea turtles to swim home and apply their experience and learning from the West to help make Chinese firms more competitive. Li is the Chairman and CEO of Wuxi PharmaTech, a global pharmaceutical, biotechnology and medical devices outsourcing company with operations in China and the US. Unlike ChemChina's Ren, who started his career scrubbing boilers, or Alibaba's Ma, who woke up early to seek practice speaking English, Li has had a relatively smooth career progression. After graduating in 1989 from Peking University, known as the "Harvard of China," he traveled to the US and earned a doctorate degree in organic chemistry at Columbia University. After graduating in 1993 he founded his first company, Pharmacopeia, a biotech firm based in New Jersey which eventually listed on the NASDAQ stock exchange.[2]

In 1999, Li received an invitation from his alma mater, Peking University, to travel to Beijing to introduce advanced Western pharmaceutical production techniques to a group of government leaders from China's Ministry of Health. Through this experience, Li saw there was a huge gap in capabilities between China's nascent pharmaceutical firms and their counterparts in the West. In addition, China was preparing to enter the World Trade Organization (WTO) in 2001. It would be vital for the officials he met from the Ministry of Health, and for the Chinese government, to ensure that Chinese pharmaceutical firms could compete with the Western companies that would surely enter China following accession to the WTO.

Li left Pharmacopeia and returned to China in 2000 to build what would become Wuxi PharmaTech. Over the course of the next eight years, he applied his experience and education from the West to create a world-class medical research and development outsourcing firm based in Shanghai. By 2008, Wuxi PharmaTech was preparing for its first overseas acquisition in the United States. In January of that year, the firm agreed to buy Saint Paul, Minnesota-based AppTec Laboratory Services for $151 million. The deal marked the largest overseas acquisition of an American company by a Chinese firm since Lenovo acquired IBM's personal computing division in 2005. The deal went smoothly through the regulatory process in China;

Wuxi PharmaTech had $200 million in cash on hand and did not have to do any financing to complete the transaction. The combined firm now has operations in China and six cities across the United States, with its US subsidiaries operating under the name Wuxi AppTec.[3]

China's go out policy

Wuxi PharmaTech's Li was wise to return to China when he did. He knew from meeting the Ministry of Health leadership in Beijing that the government planned a strong emphasis on developing the domestic healthcare and pharmaceutical sector in the years ahead. By aligning his company with government policy to develop biotechnology as a strategic emerging industry, Wuxi PharmaTech received support and recognition from the highest levels of Chinese leadership despite its status as a private firm. In March 2013, Li Keqiang even visited the firm's Shanghai headquarters[4] – just days after he had been formally appointed Chinese Premier.

The healthcare industry, and biotechnology in particular, are among the strategic emerging industries the Chinese government has targeted for the development of globally competitive firms. In October 2010, the Chinese government formally codified its intention to develop seven "strategic emerging industries" through a decision by the State Council. The strategic emerging industries include: energy efficient and environmental technologies, next generation information technology, biotechnology, high-end equipment manufacturing, new energy, new materials and new-energy vehicles. In 2010, these industries contributed less than 4 percent of China's GDP, but the government has set targets for this figure to reach 8 percent of GDP by 2015 and 15 percent by 2020. Companies in these industries received $600 billion in investment from the Chinese government over the first five years following the announced focus on strategic industry development.[5]

The "going out" policy remains the primary policy framework through which the government supports Chinese overseas investment. It was formally launched in 2000 during the 10th 5-year plan. China manages

Table 2.1   Summary table: motivations for going global

Government motivations	Business motivations
Invest foreign exchange reserves outside of China	Acquire new and advanced technologies
Secure natural resources critical for the Chinese economy	Develop global managerial talent
Create "national champions" to boost economic influence and soft power	Gain access to international brands Geographic diversification

its economic development through a series of "5-year plans" which is the Party's method of state-directed economic planning first instituted in 1953. Since 2000, companies like ChemChina and Sinopec have benefited from low-interest loans, subsidies and other forms of government support to gain access to the world's markets. SOEs were not the only firms to benefit, as large private and hybrid firms also received support to "go out" from state banks like the China Development Bank and China Export-Import Bank. Through consolidated efforts from the National Development and Reform Commission (NDRC), the China Development Bank and other actors, Chinese government bodies help to promote Chinese firms expanding overseas. Additionally, some major municipalities like Shanghai have their own schemes to promote foreign investment through municipal agencies like the Shanghai Foreign Investment Development Board, which has global offices across the US and the EU.

Government motivations

The Chinese government seeks to achieve three main goals through its go out policy. First, the government wants to invest its massive foreign reserves overseas to support China's stable long-term development. Second, it needs to strategically secure natural resources to support China's continued economic growth. Third, it aims to create "national champions" to boost its economic influence and soft power in the international marketplace. In addition to these government goals, there is a separate set of business motivations explaining why Chinese companies expand overseas, which is discussed in the second half of this chapter.

Ever since China began opening up to the world in 1978, it has attracted investment from Western companies seeking access to cheaper production capabilities and China's huge potential domestic consumer market. Yet following China's 2001 accession to the WTO, as billions of dollars of foreign investment poured in, there was strikingly little attention paid to outbound direct investment from Chinese firms. While small-scale Chinese traders operating through diaspora networks had long been active, larger Chinese firms did not start to invest overseas in earnest until the early 1990s. At that time, outward investment averaged only about $2 billion per year.[6] Given China's size and its growing stockpile of inbound investment dollars, this amount appears almost insignificant. One important reason for this was the Chinese government's caution in not allowing money to flow freely out of China's borders. Its goals were twofold: to ensure its foreign exchange reserves could stay at stable levels, and to minimize China's increasing economic dependence on overseas dollars.

From the 1990s through the first years of the 21st century, Chinese firms began to invest overseas in greater numbers to fulfill growing consumer demand in China and to invest in natural resources. By 2005, the first high-profile private sector overseas deal occurred when Lenovo purchased IBM's personal computer division for $1.25 billion.[7] One year later, Chinese outbound investment had nearly doubled from 12 billion in 2005 to 21 billion in 2006. As Figure 2.1 illustrates, China's outward investment has been growing substantially ever since.[8]

What the graph also shows is that there is still a significant gap between the inbound investments China receives from other nations and the amount it invests abroad. Contrary to popular belief, China is far from "buying up the world." Compared to the size of China's economy, at the time of writing, Chinese outward investment is relatively minor. Medium-sized economies like Belgium and the Netherlands have larger annual outflows of foreign direct investment relative to the size of their economies. As of 2013,

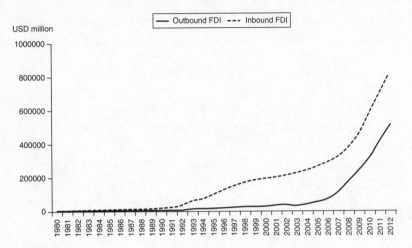

FIGURE 2.1 China's Inbound vs Outbound FDI, 1980–2012
Source: Author's image, UNCTAD data.

Chinese investment in the EU and in the US accounts for only .2 percent of their respective total FDI inflows. However, China's contribution to FDI in the West is set to increase dramatically in the years to come. For now, what is significant is the rate at which Chinese investment is increasing, the growing diversity of sectors and geographies that it is occurring in, and the large number of high-profile overseas investment deals made by Chinese companies.

> Contrary to popular belief, China is far from "buying up the world."

Money out of China

As of 2014, China has over three trillion US dollars in foreign currency reserves. How did it get there? Consumers in the West spent decades purchasing electronics, apparel, and a wide range of "Made in China" goods. Products produced in China remained cheap in part because the Chinese government deliberately undervalued its currency to keep its exports competitively priced. As a result, China has run a growing trade surplus, in which its exports have greatly exceeded its imports. When Chinese firms earn US dollars as a result of doing business with the West, the People's Bank of China (China's central bank) buys back the dollars in exchange for Chinese *renminbi*. Chinese companies are required to exchange their foreign currency for Chinese *renminbi* under a so-called "surrender requirement." China's export-led growth model has led it to accumulate large foreign exchange reserves.[9] While growing foreign exchange reserves are a positive asset, they also put inflationary pressures on the *renminbi* which the Chinese government is keen to mitigate, especially given its concerns about social stability. But now that China has all of these dollars, it needs to find a strategic way to make use of the funds in international markets, a way which is not just risky investment.

Here is a simple illustration of how China controls its foreign currency reserves (Figure 2.2).

As China strives to move beyond a growth model based on manufacturing, it has sought to become a net exporter of capital to enable more balanced long-term development. Arthur Kroeber, Managing Director at GaveKal Dragonomics, a Beijing-based consulting firm, explains: "Initially, supporting state-owned firms to invest globally was the main method of using China's foreign exchange reserves. Economically, this was strategic because it helped to support the move away from manufacturing and promote a more balanced economic growth model, while at the same time enabling Chinese firms to gain experience overseas and become more globally competitive. Politically, it was strategic because state-owned firms, particularly in the natural resource industries, became better positioned globally to secure the raw material inputs needed for China's rapid economic growth."[10]

Secure natural resources

According to the World Bank, China leads the world in total demand for major metals – copper, aluminum, nickel, tin, lead and zinc – and alone

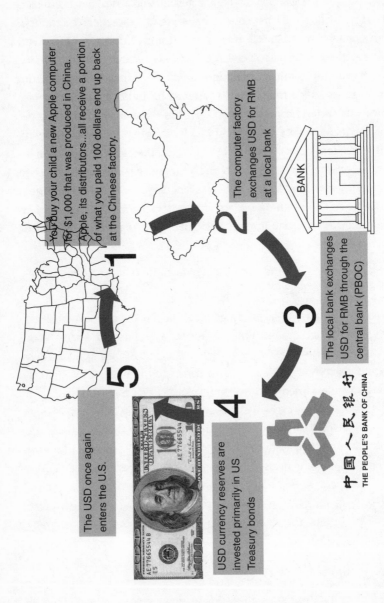

FIGURE 2.2 How China controls its foreign currency reserves

Source: Author's own image based on Thompson, Derek. "Infographic: How China Manipulates Its Currency." *The Atlantic.* March 2011.

Image text:

1 — You buy your child a new Apple computer for $1,000 that was produced in China. Apple, its distributors...all receive a portion of what you paid 100 dollars end up back at the Chinese factory.

2 — The computer factory exchanges USD for RMB at a local bank

BANK

3 — The local bank exchanges USD for RMB through the central bank (PBOC)

中国人民银行
THE PEOPLE'S BANK OF CHINA

4 — USD currency reserves are invested primarily in US Treasury bonds

5 — The USD once again enters the U.S.

consumes nearly a quarter of world production. China has also become the world's largest official trader of timber and wood products, much of it sourced from the developing world. Wendy Leutert, a Cornell PhD who specializes in Chinese overseas investment, explains: "China's soaring consumption of natural resources has transformed natural resource extraction and trade in the developing world, particularly in Africa and Latin America. But economic investment has not always translated easily into political influence, and Chinese firms have faced mounting challenges in their relationships with actors on the ground."[11] Domestic demand has driven a growing number of deals by Chinese firms in developing countries including Peru, Venezuela, Kenya and Nigeria as well as in developed countries like Australia, Canada and the United States. This approach enables China to invest its foreign exchange reserves to secure the natural resources its economy needs, and to profit by selling them in international markets as well.

In addition to capital outflows, Western scholars and journalists have written detailed accounts about Chinese firms "exporting" entire labor forces from China together with sub-standard labor practices. Chinese workers are the face of China's expanded economic stakes in the developing world, where youth populations in many countries are growing and unemployment remains a serious problem. In many developing countries, skilled and literate workers may be scarce and command higher salaries. Particularly in high-technology industries like mining or oil refining, or for technical or management positions, it may make sense for Chinese firms to bring highly skilled workers from China. But arguments for the importation of Chinese labor become especially difficult to defend for industries like construction or agriculture in countries with ample supplies of low-skilled labor. However, Deborah Brautigam, professor at the School of Advanced International Studies at Johns Hopkins University, argues that the real story is far more complicated. Based on extensive fieldwork and research, she notes that she has not encountered a Chinese company in Africa that has hired an entirely Chinese labor force.[12]

Soft power

The public image of Chinese firms in the Western countries where they invest strongly affects how China itself is perceived. This is especially the case for state-owned enterprises, given their close relationship with the Chinese state and their large size and high profile abroad. Perceptions of China can be negatively affected if Chinese firms are criticized for labor rights violations or environmental damage. Chinese firms have also been critiqued for their investments outside of the West, for example for doing business with unsavoury regimes in countries like Sudan, Iran, and North Korea. But on the other hand, China's image may receive a positive boost if its investment leads to job growth and tax dollars. The increasing number of Chinese firms joining the ranks of the Fortune Global 500 – 95 firms as of 2013[13] – reflects well on both Chinese industry and China's ability to create globally competitive firms. At the same time, it also highlights China's growing economic, political, and cultural influence. International image and the expansion of "soft power" is a key consideration in China's going out strategy.

What is "soft power"? Joseph Nye, Harvard University professor and former dean of the Kennedy School of Government, coined the phrase in his famous 1990 *Foreign Policy* article of the same name. According to Nye: "Power is the ability to alter the behavior of others to get what you want. There are basically three ways to do that: coercion (sticks), payments (carrots), and attraction (soft power)." Nye further explained that a nation has three main sources of soft power: "its culture (in places where it is attractive to others), its political values (when it lives up to them at home and abroad), and its foreign policies (when they are seen as legitimate and having moral authority)."[14] The soft power element of China's going out strategy is critical to understanding why Chinese firms go global. Through creating "national champions" in the corporate realm, companies that earn the respect and admiration of their Western competitors, China itself is viewed as a "higher value" nation.

The desire to create "national champions" is shared by actors at the national level all the way down to the executives themselves who lead Chinese firms. Many of these executives have a strong sense of patriotic pride and want to make China shine on the international stage. Yuan Haiying, a former Chinese government official and President of government relations consultancy Yuan Associates, explains: "Chinese businesspeople have a dream. Their dream is to create firms with the brand recognition of a General Electric or a Google. By doing so they will advance the role of China in the global economy and improve perceptions of China as a whole."[15] Moreover from a strategic perspective, these executives recognize that framing their companies as "national champions" will help them to garner public support and resources. This is particularly important given increasing concerns among Chinese citizens about the lack of transparency and potential for corruption within state-owned industry.

> International image and the expansion of "soft power" is a key consideration in China's going out strategy.

The business motivations

To move up the value chain and become globally competitive, Chinese companies are driven by four main business motivations: the acquisition of new and advanced technologies; development of global managerial talent; gaining access to international brands; and geographic diversification.

Advanced technology

Wu Gang, CEO of wind-turbine manufacturer Goldwind, is from Xinjiang province in far western China. Xinjiang is unique among other provinces in China because it sits at the intersection of Chinese, Central Asian, and Middle Eastern cultures. In contrast to the Han Chinese who comprise the vast majority of China's population, Xinjiang's native Uyghur people are of Turkic origin. But during the past thirty years, massive waves of government-encouraged Han migration have transformed the economy and the demography of China's western border regions. In 1949, Han Chinese represented less than 7 percent of Xinjiang's population (220,000 Han Chinese).[16] By 2008, Han Chinese migration to the remote region jumped dramatically to constitute 40 percent of the province's population (8.4 million Han Chinese). With rapid industrialization transforming Xinjiang's rugged geography, Wu worked to bring clean energy to one of the last environmentally pristine parts of China.

By the late 1980s, European engineers were already traveling to Xinjiang to test their wind turbines. It was a perfect opportunity for Wu, an engineer, to learn from top global talent. After learning the "ins and outs" of the wind-turbine industry in Xinjiang, Wu received an offer in 1997 from state science officials to build a 600-kilowatt wind turbine in China. From this humble beginning, Wu's firm Goldwind now competes with major industry players such as Denmark's Vestas, Germany's Siemens and the United States' General Electric. But in the 1990's, Wu and his firm were just getting started. Goldwind began looking overseas to identify a potential partner with the right technology. Initially it partnered with Germany's Jacobs Energie, but early attempts to apply Jacobs' technology in China failed. Wu discovered that possessing international designs and successfully applying international manufacturing processes are very different. Given its limited experience, Goldwind struggled to manufacture Jacobs-designed windmills effectively. In an interview with *The New Yorker*, Wu was quoted as saying his firm's application of Jacobs' technology was a "terrible failure ... whole blades dropped off ... it was really dangerous."[17]

By 2004, Goldwind identified a new German partner – Vensys. The two companies spent a total of three years partnering on a range of projects and research and development initiatives. Through this process, the companies found great synergy between their businesses; so much so that in 2007, Goldwind acquired a 70 percent stake in Vensys for €41 million ($53 million).[18] While the acquisition itself was relatively small, it gave Goldwind access to advanced German technology and the ability to compete successfully in Western wind energy markets. In 2012,

Wu explained that going into developed markets first was critical for Goldwind's long-term success. The West offered Goldwind an environment with stricter safety standards and product requirements than in China. The advanced operating environment helped Goldwind in two ways: "First, it helped with the maturation of our company. Second, it helped improve our overall competitiveness as a firm."

Why do Chinese companies buy technology?

A December 2009 article by Evan Osnos in *The New Yorker* featured Goldwind as a key player in the development of Chinese technology firms. It described how a group of China's most prestigious scientists wrote a letter to Deng Xiaoping in March 1986 warning him that China was falling behind globally in technology. They called for China to launch a *xin jishu geming* (新技术革命): "a new technological revolution." Osnos declared this was China's "Sputnik moment," as Deng fervently agreed and engineered government programs to funnel domestic and foreign investment into technology research. From this "new technological revolution," Goldwind Science and Technology Company was born.[19]

As Chapter 1 introduced, the delineation between publicly owned and private firms is not as clear in China as it is in the West. While most firms would have crumbled after the failed Jacobs Energie partnership, Goldwind received enough support from the Chinese government to continue operating until it established its successful relationship with Vensys. But while government support enabled Goldwind to survive, it was not in itself enough to make it globally competitive. The number one reason why Chinese firms partner with foreign firms and strive to enter developed economies is to secure advanced technology unavailable in China.

Chinese firms have often built their core business by relying on technologies and systems that are generations older than those available in advanced economies. In the beginning, Goldwind did not need "the best" technology, it just needed "good enough" technology that was better than anything its competitors in China had access to. This explains why Jacobs initially appeared to be an attractive partner. Such technology allows Chinese firms to gain initial scale in China, but as reputation and market share grow, domestic competitors quickly emerge. Competitors also gain access to the same level of technology and initiate a price war. At this stage, firms compete exclusively on price – cutting away at each other's margins until the profitability of everyone's businesses is in jeopardy.

Chinese firms able to move beyond joint ventures at home and go overseas to acquire advanced technology through mergers and acquisitions or investment can break this cycle – at least temporarily. Instead of competing on ever-decreasing profit margins, with the latest technology from the West they are able to offer a better product or service than their domestic competitors at a higher profit per unit. Through the Vensys acquisition, Goldwind acquired technology that helped separate it from the majority of its domestic competitors. By acquiring advanced technology overseas, the Chinese firm obtains a competitive advantage over its domestic counterparts in markets at home and abroad.

International managerial talent

The second reason why Chinese firms "go out" to become more competitive is to build experienced managerial talent and incorporate international best practices. This global perspective might come from a "sea turtle" with decades of experience doing business overseas, or from a proven international manager with little to no experience doing business with Chinese firms. Sea turtles are often the preferred way for Chinese companies to build their overseas management capacity because of shared language and cultural backgrounds. However, in the case of cross-border acquisitions, a Chinese firm may not always have a choice between returned Chinese managers accustomed to China and Western executives who are not.

This was the case when Lenovo purchased IBM's personal computing division in 2005. The Lenovo–IBM acquisition is one of the most cited cases on the topic of Chinese businesses going global. And why wouldn't it be? The story of an emerging Chinese technology giant purchasing a division of an American blue chip multinational was an almost unheard-of development at the time. Most accounts of the acquisition focus on the technology aspect or the brand acquisition element of the deal. Both were important factors in Lenovo's decision to purchase IBM's ThinkPad line, but it is striking that very few accounts focus on the global managerial talent to which Lenovo gained access through the acquisition.

Margaret Wei, a psychologist with a PhD from Harvard, reflects on her time working with Lenovo after its purchase of IBM's personal computing division. Dr. Wei started consulting for Lenovo in 2006 while working with an established consulting firm and later joined Lenovo to help manage the cultural integration between the Western and Chinese senior management. With an influx of Western talent into Lenovo as a result of the acquisition, the company needed support merging their two corporate cultures into a shared global Lenovo culture. Dr. Wei brought the cross-cultural perspective that the company needed. Leveraging her experience in both the US and China along with her doctorate in psychology, she set to work to help both sides understand each other's perspective. When Bill Amelio, President and CEO of Lenovo at the time, assessed the capabilities of his Chinese senior management team, he was shocked at how few team members he felt were actually able to manage a global business. There were some that he wanted to fire immediately and others who he wanted to demote until they gained the necessary experience to re-join the senior leadership team.

According to Dr. Wei, if top leaders lost their "Senior Vice President (SVP)" title, it would be an extreme "loss of face" that would not only damage the demoted employees' loyalty, but would likely lead to attrition across the management team. Face or *mianzi* (面子), as it is known in Chinese, can be "given" (to praise or honor someone) or "lost" (to embarrass or criticize someone). *Mianzi* is frequently emphasized as a unique cultural element in doing business in China, but arguably few foreign executives would stick around after a major demotion, or not be offended by open criticism in an all-company meeting. To help manage the transition, Lenovo adopted an alternative solution that satisfied the needs of all parties. Rather than officially demote the senior leaders who lacked the necessary skills, two levels of SVPs were temporarily created during the integration phase. The title Senior Vice President (SVP) would be reserved for leaders who clearly were prepared to manage a global organization, while Senior Vice President 2 (SVP2) would be designated for those with skill gaps. In addition, this differentiation was entirely internal, allowing everyone to maintain "SVP" status for his or her friends, families, and contacts outside Lenovo. This management reform strategy was probably one of the most successful moves that Amelio made during his short and challenged tenure with the firm.[20] Chapter 3 analyzes in greater detail the factors that have led to Lenovo's success operating a global business.

Brand buys

The third reason why Chinese firms go global is to increase their competitiveness by gaining access to globally recognized brands. First, and most importantly, international brands benefit Chinese companies by helping to bridge the "trust gap." Consumers overseas might wonder: *I have never heard of this firm, so how can I trust that its products are of good quality or that it will fulfill its obligations as a business partner?* Consumer trust is a particularly important challenge for Chinese firms, given existing conceptions of low-quality "Made in China" products and a recent series of safety scandals. Acquiring an internationally recognized brand can help Chinese firms boost their overseas market share more quickly. Building a brand from scratch can take decades, millions of dollars and savvy public relations. Given their relative youth, Chinese firms lack the decades of international experience to have built globally recognized brands through their own efforts. The next best alternative to investing hundreds of millions of dollars in marketing may be to buy another firm's long-term established brand in the same industry.

Chapter 4 provides detailed analysis into Chinese firms' ability to build global brands and offers a series of suggestions for how they can do so. It introduces the story of Tong Zhicheng and his piano company Pearl River Piano. Tong adopted a successful strategy of acquiring a respected piano brand from Germany to gain access to the US market where the German firm already had a reputation for high quality. At the same time, Tong began to market Pearl River branded pianos alongside the German brand to gradually build his firm's reputation in its overseas markets. Through its successful brand acquisition strategy, Pearl River became the world's largest piano manufacturer.

Acquiring established international brands helps Chinese firms to fill trust gaps at home as well as in Western markets. Bright Dairy illustrates how acquiring a trusted international brand can bolster – or in this case, rebuild – a Chinese firm's consumer trust and competitiveness. In 2008, several of China's top dairy producers were accused of adding the chemical melamine to artificially raise their products' protein levels. Consumers in China were horrified, especially Chinese families who do their utmost to ensure their children receive the best food, medical care and education that they can afford. In the wake of the 2008 scandal, Chinese consumers lost faith in the entire dairy industry. Demand for foreign milk powder has soared as Chinese parents go to great lengths to procure it. In 2013, Hong Kong issued a new law restricting anyone from taking more than two cans of milk powder outside of Hong Kong. The law was prompted by a milk powder shortage caused by excessive exportation by mainland Chinese visitors and grey market suppliers.

During the 2008 scandal, Bright Dairy was one of the most widely publicized violators. In 2008 its losses amounted to nearly $42 million, with company revenues down 234 percent from the year prior.[21] To earn trust back from Chinese consumers, Wang Zongnan, Chairman of Bright Food, sought to establish relationships with secure and trusted dairy suppliers in New Zealand. By partnering with a trusted international brand name, Wang wanted to prove to consumers that his firm had dramatically transformed its production practices and consumer safety standards. The best way to do this was to identify a premium international brand that could be imported and used directly in China. In 2010, Bright Food purchased a 51 percent stake in New Zealand's Synliat Milk for $58 million.[22] In a statement issued by the Chinese firm following the deal: "The international reputation and consumer recognition of New Zealand's dairy products are beneficial for our company to enter the premium infant formula market."

Chapter 4 assesses in more detail whether or not Chinese firms are capable of building their own global brands, and the challenges they face.

> Chinese firms often "go out" to secure new and advanced technologies, incorporate global managerial talent, gain access to international brands and to diversify into new geographies.

Geographic diversification

After decades of suppressed entrepreneurship and market development, China's economy has grown consistently at almost double-digit rates. In the euphoric atmosphere of the early reform and opening period, Chinese companies grew at exponential rates and their stakeholders grew accustomed to unsustainable levels of performance. Today, Chinese firms face rising labor costs and industries often crowded with foreign as well as domestic competitors. The current business environment is far less favorable and companies' growth and profits are no longer assured. Many Chinese companies now find themselves confronting the "law of large numbers."

The "law of large numbers"[23] refers to the situation when a Chinese company reaches a certain size and it becomes difficult or impossible to sustain earlier levels of growth. To continue producing historic growth numbers, a firm must choose from one or more of the following three options:

1. Acquire a company
2. Diversify into new business lines
3. Diversify into new geographies

The first option is the easiest to understand: by acquiring an existing company, the Chinese buyer grows larger by incorporating the new business into its existing operations. Many state-owned firms grew by mandatory acquisition of smaller failing SOEs. Today, private firms too are pursuing acquisitions as part of a structured business strategy to expand their scale. The second option is to diversify into new business lines, either through acquisitions or directly. As demonstrated by the case of ChemChina in Chapter 1, Chinese firms can grow by expanding horizontally and entering new market segments that are either in line with their existing business focus or vastly different – like a chemical company operating a fast food noodle chain. The third growth path for Chinese companies is to enter new geographical areas overseas. New geographical areas represent new potential markets for goods and services that Chinese firms are already producing for domestic consumers.

While Chinese companies going global face a variety of business risks, overseas expansion enables them to mitigate dependence on the China market alone. The Chinese government's massive $586 billion stimulus package in 2008[24] enabled China to weather the global financial crisis far better than Western economies. However, the long-term sustainability of economic growth driven by government stimulus is questionable. Infrastructure and construction, both core industries for stimulus spending, will need to identify new sources of growth outside China to ensure its businesses continue to thrive. Rising competition, inflation, and labor costs have also challenged Chinese firms to look outside of China to mitigate their risk. According to Kaiser Kuo,[25] Head of International Communications for Chinese Internet giant Baidu: "If you were to poll our analysts, you would find some who would rather not see us go global for fear that it would take our attention off the prize at home. But eventually, Baidu has to go global – the domestic market, while still enormous, will eventually see slowing growth. Diversification into other markets is inevitable and there's no time like the present to begin the push. If we do things right, I believe that a significant portion of our future revenues will come from abroad."

Zoomlion, China's second largest heavy machinery manufacturer after Sany Heavy, is actively seeking access to new markets overseas as profit margins in China shrink. After the infrastructure boom fueled by Chinese government stimulus spending began to wind down, Zoomlion and Sany experienced a dramatic slowdown in their businesses. Expanding into new markets overseas became a critical part of both companies' strategies to sustain business growth. In 2008, Zoomlion along with a consortium of investors including Goldman Sachs purchased Italian concrete machinery producer Compagnia Italiana Forme Acciaio SpA (CIFA) for $215 million (€163 million). In 2012, Sany purchased a 90 percent stake in German industrial firm Putzmeister for $475 million (€360 million). Zoomlion's Vice-President of overseas business, He Wenjin, was quoted in 2012: "We hope that our business in overseas markets will contribute 30 percent of our total annual revenue by 2015, up from less than 10 percent now."[26] For Zoomlion and its executive leaders, a dual strategy of overseas growth in both developed and emerging markets will help it reach this goal.

Key takeaways from this chapter

Chinese companies are expanding into overseas markets at record rates. Chinese outbound investment increased from $20 billion in 2006 to $70 billion in 2012 – an increase of 250 percent. Outbound investment from China continues to increase at extraordinary rates each year. However, China is not "buying up the world's corporations." China's total outward investment as a percentage of its GDP is relatively insignificant in comparison to smaller nations like Belgium and the Netherlands with larger outward investments flows. What is significant, however, is the substantial year-on-year growth of Chinese overseas direct investment, along with the shift in its focus beyond simply resources to industries like consumer goods, manufacturing, and entertainment. The US and EU's slow recovery from the global financial crisis has undoubtedly expedited the frequency and scale of Chinese companies' investments overseas. But the rise of these firms beyond the walls of the Middle Kingdom was bound to happen due to underlying government and business motivations.

China's "going out" strategy is motivated by both political and economic considerations. Politically, it enables the government to secure the natural resources necessary to fuel China's rapid economic growth.

Internationalization of the state-owned sector provides the Chinese government with a channel to invest its vast foreign exchange reserves while boosting long-term economic growth. The development of national champions in strategic industries helps China expand its influence through soft power by entering our daily lives around the world. This does not mean that Chinese companies "going West" is part of a grand strategy by the government to infiltrate or influence Western society. The business case for Chinese companies to "go out" is very strong. The domestic market is fiercely competitive and Chinese firms require advanced technology and global management best practices to stay ahead of competitors back home. Global brands help bridge the trust gap for Chinese companies seeking to connect with an international audience for the first time, or rebrand their firm as a high-end alternative for the domestic Chinese market. Most importantly, international expansion opens new markets to grow Chinese firms' businesses and to become less reliant on a slowing Chinese economy.

The motivations introduced in this chapter for international expansion present a clear argument for why Chinese companies want to go West. But it takes more than desire alone to build a successful international business. Chinese companies have comparatively fewer years of operational experience than their counterparts in the West, and they have even less experience operating in markets outside China. *Are Chinese companies ready to take the leap overseas?* Chapter 3 takes up this critical question.

chapter 3

The Unprepared: Are Chinese Companies Prepared to Go West?

Li Ning had the weight of a nation on his shoulders at the 1988 Summer Olympic Games in Seoul, Korea. He was a national hero after winning three gold medals in gymnastics at China's first summer Olympics appearance four years earlier in Los Angeles. Unlike today's China, which topped the gold medal count at the 2008 Beijing Olympics and came in second at the 2012 London Olympics, Li Ning's achievements in 1984 were remarkable for a nation new to the Olympic stage. Unfortunately, Li Ning faltered at the Seoul Games and did not win a single medal. Deeply disappointed, Li Ning felt he was returning home a national disappointment rather than a national hero. Doing everything he could to avoid media scrutiny, Li Ning wandered around South Korea's Kimpo International Airport searching for a moment of solitude. By chance he bumped into another famous "Li" – Li Jingwei, founder of Jianlibao Group, China's most famous beverage brand and sports drink maker. Li Jingwei encouraged Li Ning to think seriously about the next stage in his career. As a former Olympic gold medalist, Li Ning would still have plenty of opportunities to be sponsored by Chinese brands, but Li Jingwei convinced Li Ning that the Olympic gymnast himself had enough brand power to build his own company.

After announcing his retirement from professional gymnastics later that year, Li Ning went to work for Li Jingwei at Jianlibao Group. Li Jingwei helped Li Ning secure investment to launch his own athletic apparel firm, which began as part of Jianlibao, but eventually spun off as the independent company Li-Ning in 1994. As an independent businessman, Li Ning studied Chinese Communist Party founder Mao Zedong's successful strategy of *nongcun baowei chengshi* (农村包围城市), or "surrounding the cities from the countryside." By winning over rural areas first, Li Ning hoped that his company could then take on the competition in major cities. His firm followed this path to commercial success, gaining brand recognition in China's second and third tier cities and then moving successfully into major metropolises like Beijing, Shanghai and Guangzhou.

By the 2008 Beijing Olympics, Li-Ning ranked as the second largest athletic brand in all of China – second only to Nike and followed by Adidas. Founder Li Ning rose back to Olympic glory as he lit the official Games cauldron for the world to see during the opening ceremonies. But rather than focusing on dethroning Nike as the number one athletic brand in China, Li-Ning decided to take on Nike in the US. Unfortunately for Li-Ning, this move proved premature. David Wolf, Managing Director of Allison+Partners' Global China Practice recalled: "Just when Li-Ning should have been using its local advantage to secure the home field against foreign competitors Nike and Adidas, it began turning its attention away."[1] In 2010 the firm began to compete with Nike in the US and officially opened its US headquarters and first retail store in Portland, Oregon. But both the store and Li-Ning USA's overall business strategy were flawed from the outset.

Li-Ning failed to understand how to effectively develop and manage the key relationships necessary to Chinese companies going West. As a consumer goods company, Li-Ning's overseas expansion plans faced little scrutiny from American regulators. The marketing of basketball sneakers and badminton rackets was not about to cause uproar on Capitol Hill. However, Li-Ning may have overestimated the amount of local government support the city of Portland and state of Oregon could provide. Chinese firms like Li-Ning that enter the US for the first time often expect government relations to be closely linked to business success, as is the case back home. But once they arrive, these firms face the harsh reality that there is a set of standard business rules applicable to everyone. Instead of cultivating government support, all they can do is pay specialized third parties in the tax, legal and business advisory industries to help them navigate the new market – the government is only there to collect tax dollars and ensure fair play.

In addition, Li-Ning failed to manage its US employees effectively. At the time of Li-Ning's entry into the US market, its entire US operations only employed 28 people. With such a small team on the ground in the US, most decisions about the company's strategy were made at the Chinese headquarters rather than at the local office in Oregon, leaving limited decision-making authority for the American managers. Mark McMillan, former director of design engineering, was one of the founding team members. In September 2010, one and a half years after McMillan started working for Li-Ning, his US-based boss offered him a promotion to a global product development role based in Beijing. However, the Beijing management team did not agree with the decision and withdrew the offer two months after McMillan had accepted the job and when his promotion had already been communicated to his colleagues in Oregon. McMillan went on to sue Li-Ning for "calling him derogatory names and rescinding a promised promotion" in a drawn out three-year-long court case which he won and in which he was awarded $1.25 million.[2] Less than two years after McMillan's promotion had been revoked, Li-Ning halved its staff from 30 employees to 15 and it became clear that the management was preparing to shut down its US operations. Li-Ning's mismanagement of its employees on the ground in the US generated too much focus on internal strife rather than on business execution.

But the most striking misstep in Li-Ning's first attempt to enter the US market was its failure to understand American consumers. A 2010 *TIME* magazine article described the incongruity of Li-Ning's product offering with the American athletic apparel market. It noted: "The products in the Portland store do not shy away from Li-Ning's origins, highlighting apparel for popular sports in China like badminton, table tennis and kung fu – games you won't find front and center at nearby Niketown."[3] The one exception in their product portfolio was basketball sneakers, but even there Li-Ning missed an opportunity to connect with American consumers. Li-Ning chose to sponsor NBA athlete Baron Davis as the face of its basketball apparel in the US, but Davis was far from a famous player in the league. Li-Ning's competitors like Adidas or Nike sponsored several far more popular NBA athletes to promote their basketball sneakers, including NBA champion Kobe Bryant and slam dunk champion Dwight Howard.

Furthermore, the Li-Ning USA team did not receive nearly enough investment from its Chinese headquarters to support its entry into the US market. To compete with Nike and other competitors in the US, Li-Ning would have needed a far larger team and millions of dollars in marketing budget to build its brand. Brian Cupp, who was brand initiative director for basketball at the time, felt that Li-Ning was well positioned to make the right investments in its American business since the firm had a dominant market position back home. He remarked in a 2010 interview: "Because we have such a strong foundation of a business in China, I think that gives us an opportunity to be very aggressive and take some risks here where maybe others can't because they are so reliant here in the US."[4] What Cupp failed to mention was that the Beijing headquarters didn't allow the American arm to take the necessary financial risks to be successful, and the investments that it did make were disastrous. One example was the company's joint sponsorship of several marathons in which its partner went bankrupt and had to sell off its Li-Ning running shoe inventory at steep discounts.[5] Given such limited resources, the Li-Ning USA office could not effectively build its brand, especially when the only press it did receive from the American media was negative.

Within less than three years of operations, Li-Ning closed its store in Portland and returned to China to make up lost ground against Nike and Adidas as well as an emerging Chinese competitor, Anta. While Li-Ning's first attempt to go West was a commercial failure, its mistakes provide valuable lessons for other Chinese companies looking to avoid similar pitfalls.

Learning how to go West

Li-Ning's first attempt to enter the US market demonstrates that as much as Chinese firms aspire to go global, they may not be prepared for the challenges they will encounter. The incompatibility of Li-Ning's product offering for American consumers, its mismanagement of overseas staff, and the firm's lack of a sound investment and marketing strategy left the firm with a loss in the US and on the defensive back home. Are Chinese companies like Li-Ning ready to "go West" and expand into developed markets? News of Chinese firms' international deals in the *Financial Times* and the *Wall Street Journal* might suggest the answer is a simple: "Yes." However, it takes more than aspirations and investment to succeed overseas in the long-term. The vast majority of Chinese firms – private, hybrid, and state-owned – are not yet ready to compete internationally.

> The vast majority of Chinese firms are not yet ready to compete internationally.

In 2009, then Vice-Premier Wang Qishan acknowledged this himself. He challenged Chinese firms with global aspirations: "You think acquiring an overseas firm is simply a matter of money? Can you integrate it? Can you actually manage it?"[6] Chinese state and hybrid firms possess a range of advantages to support their international expansion efforts. For example, they have relatively easy access to financing for investment projects and seemingly guaranteed government bailouts and absorption of losses when investments go awry. But while overall most Chinese companies are not yet ready to compete successfully in Western markets, that does not mean they should not enter them. The only way for Chinese firms to build the necessary understanding and capabilities to compete internationally is to gain first-hand exposure, and to learn from the experiences of other Chinese companies that took the leap before them.

The five key relationships needed to go West

One way to understand how Chinese companies can best prepare themselves to succeed globally is through a conceptual framework based on the relationships they need to master. In *Billions*, Tom Doctoroff frames his analysis of Chinese consumer culture around the Confucian concept of *wulun* (五伦), the five key relationships that structured traditional Chinese society. Under the five relationships, people's roles and responsibilities were strictly defined depending on who they interacted with. An individual's role and responsibilities varied according to whether the relationship was between: (i) ruler to ruled, (ii) father to son, (iii) husband to wife, (iv) older brother to younger brother, or (v) friend to friend.[7]

Extending this conceptual framework to Chinese companies expanding overseas suggests there are five key relationships they must get right. These relationships are: (i) company to government, (ii) company to employees, (iii) company to customers, (iv) company to community, and (v) company to capital (Table 3.1). But while each of these relationships is important to Chinese firms' overall success abroad, most Chinese companies do not do a good job of managing all five. In addition to the typical challenges faced by any company expanding into a new country,

Table 3.1 The five key relationships needed to go West

i. Company to government
ii. Company to employees
iii. Company to customers
iv. Company to community
v. Company to capital

Chinese firms also face unique obstacles. By learning how to overcome them, Chinese firms can successfully implement best practices to globalize their businesses while becoming responsible, competitive multinational corporations.

Relationship 1: company to government

Any company expanding into a new country should first conduct a detailed assessment of the overall business environment prior to market entry. Based on their company's product or service, such research can help to identify the overall size of the market, its stability, and the potential for long-term growth. Before investing in a foreign market, firms may produce or commission reports on the business and regulatory environment, political risk concerns, and key influencers on the ground. Even if companies conduct market assessments and due diligence work up front, they will nearly always encounter unexpected challenges related to local government and regulatory policies.

For Chinese companies, failure to understand local regulations and the varying roles played by government – at home in Beijing and in host investment countries – often proves extremely challenging as they expand into new markets overseas. Government relations are very important for Chinese companies prior to their going overseas, and once they begin operating in the target country.

Relationship with the Chinese government

Chinese companies preparing to go overseas need to develop and maintain relationships with domestic authorities in each of the government agencies introduced in Chapter 1. Executives – particularly those in private or hybrid firms without strong government ties – often have a hard time assessing which Chinese government actors possess regulatory authority over their intended investment and what the appropriate procedure is to apply for investment approval. In 2013, the European Union Chamber of Commerce in China (EUROCHAM) published a study titled *Chinese Outbound Investment in the European Union*, in which it surveyed 74

Chinese executives representing firms with at least one investment in an EU country. Respondents urged the Chinese government to "provide more convenient outbound investment procedures. The Ministry of Commerce (MOFCOM), State Administration of Foreign Exchange (SAFE) and other relevant authorities should provide integrated services." The report also expressed the executives' desire for the Chinese government to "provide more room for companies to make decisions; the current multi-level approvals are way too complicated."[8]

The complex process of overseas investment approval, which varies depending on the size and ownership structure of the Chinese company, is difficult and cumbersome for Chinese executives to navigate for the first time. The Chinese government bodies introduced in Chapter 1 all play different roles depending on the specific deal. Involvement from any or all of the following bureaus is necessary: the National Development and Reform Commission (NDRC), the Ministry of Commerce (MOFCOM), State-Owned Assets Supervision and Administrative Commission of the State Council (SASAC), the State Administration of Foreign Exchange (SAFE), or the Ministry of Finance (MOF).

Relationship with the foreign government

Once a Chinese firm begins working with the appropriate regulators within China, it still may face obstacles from overseas governments before its investment is approved. Depending on the intended sector of its investment, a Chinese firm may encounter resistance from the overseas government if the deal is considered to pose a national security or anti-competition threat. In the US, the inter-agency Committee on Foreign Investment in the United States (CFIUS, pronounced "sifius") reviews potentially sensitive investments by foreign firms. According to CFIUS, its mandate is "to review transactions that could result in control of a US business by a foreign person … in order to determine the effect of such transactions on the national security of the United States."[9] Similarly, Australia has the Foreign Investment Review Board (FIRB) and Canada has the *Investment Canada Act,* co-managed by Industry

Canada and the Ministry of Industry. While the EU does not have a unified body that reviews proposed investments by Chinese and other international companies into the EU, most member states have their own respective review processes at the country level. Chapter 6 focuses on the potential concerns associated with Chinese investment in the West and discusses each of the investment review mechanisms listed above in more detail.

Once they arrive: navigating the local regulatory landscape

When they first enter a new country, Chinese companies do not always understand how best to engage the local government and how the local regulatory environment operates. According to the EUROCHAM survey on Chinese outbound investment in the EU, the top difficulties Chinese executives reported encountering when they began doing business in the EU derived from a lack of understanding about how to work with governments overseas and comply with local regulations. The most common operating obstacles reported were issues related to work and residence permits, labor law (unions, contracts, social security), and tax regulations and accounting. Additional reported difficulties also included a lack of support, problems communicating with local authorities, and a lack of clarity about company legal requirements (Figure 3.1).

Chinese firms encounter similar issues in the US as well. Craig Allen, Deputy Assistant Secretary for Asia at the US Department of Commerce, International Trade Administration explains: "Chinese companies are looking for guidance from the federal government to help navigate the investment environment in the United States. While there may be more autonomy for state and municipal governments to help Chinese firms invest, at the federal level ... we remain geographically neutral and do not provide Chinese firms with advice that favors one state over another."[10] Significant variation in regulations among states makes it difficult for Chinese firms investing in the US. For this reason, state governors would be wise to assemble groups of long-standing advisory firms from their states – specializing in law, tax regulations, and public relations – and go

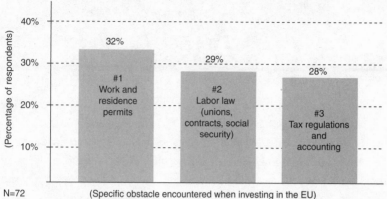

FIGURE 3.1 / Percentage of Chinese firms that encountered obstacles when investing in the EU

Source: Author's own image, European Union Chamber of Commerce in China (2013) data.

on roadshows in China to promote the available projects in their state. Indeed, states are already increasing their efforts to streamline the Chinese outbound investment process with 33 state trade offices now operating in Shanghai. Partnership with local third-party professional services firms would help Chinese companies go more smoothly from step A to Z in their US investments.

Back home, Chinese companies are accustomed to communicating closely with governments at the central, provincial and local levels. Domestic Chinese firms regularly visit government agencies to make tax payments, process paperwork and collect official red stamps for various approval letters. Depending on a company's type and size, it may even benefit from preferential agreements with the government in which it receives land, loans and other benefits. Chinese executives may be inclined to offer a government official who provides such incentives a *hongbao* (红包) or red envelope full of cash to express their gratitude for helping to set their business up for success. Such business practices may be customary in China and remain common in operations by Chinese firms in emerging markets; however, they will not work in the West.

> Chinese companies do not always understand how best to engage the local government and how the local regulatory environment operates.

Chinese companies will continue to face challenges dealing with governments and regulations in Western markets until information about how to invest in host countries is more readily accessible and regulations are better understood. Chapter 8 provides further analysis and recommendations about how Chinese companies, governments and other key stakeholders should respond to Chinese companies going West. While ties with foreign government authorities may be the first relationship Chinese firms must manage, there are others to consider. As Chinese firms operate in different cultures and hire more employees from around the world, *company to employees* is the second key relationship they must master.

Relationship 2: company to employees

Trust among members of a company team is an essential element of overseas business. Building this trust between managers and their employees in international offices is especially critical. When a company has an international organizational structure with employees across Asia, Europe, North America and Latin America, executives need to have people on the ground who they trust to carry out the company's mission. When entering a new market, most firms tend to appoint high-potential staff members who have proven themselves in the home office and demonstrated their loyalty to senior management and company values. For Chinese companies, the value of having executives in other countries from their own culture who can speak their language is even more important. For example take Pin Ni, president of North America for Wanxiang, a Chinese automotive supplier and new energy firm. Ni's strong performance at Wanxiang, together with his marriage to the Wanxiang chairman's daughter, helped him to become a highly trusted member of the global management team.[11] When managers must choose between someone they know can be trusted and someone whose qualifications alone might make them a good fit for the local business environment, they will almost always choose the individual they trust. Thus, the first employees to help a firm expand overseas are often not experts about the local business environment themselves.

Differences in degree of 'internationalization'

Many senior Chinese corporate leaders managing the operations of Chinese firms overseas have had significantly less exposure to outside cultures than their counterparts at Western firms. This is largely a legacy of China's turbulent history during the twentieth century and the decades when the country was effectively closed to the outside world. But future generations of leaders will be much more knowledgeable about international cultures, brands, and business practices. China has already surpassed Germany and the United States to officially become the world's largest outbound tourism market. Yet while the degree of internationalization of the "post 1980s" generations (Chinese born after 1980) has increased dramatically, and bodes well for future generations of Chinese business leaders, the current leadership of many Chinese firms has had limited exposure to global markets and Western corporate culture. As Margaret Wei, the psychologist who helped manage the integration between Lenovo and IBM, explains: "Global executives from the West typically have lived in multiple regions, travelled extensively, and are more culturally exposed than their Chinese counterparts."[12]

> The current leadership of many Chinese firms has had limited exposure to global markets and Western corporate culture.

Western executives can apply the understanding gained through their diverse cultural experiences to adapt their management practices in overseas business environments. Most importantly, through their extensive travel and overseas work assignments, Western managers learn that "their way" is not always the best way, and that they need to be conscious and adapt to market-specific cultural nuances overseas. For example,

Jai Thampi, head of international markets for consumer electronics firm Belkin, has worked in the Netherlands, France, Germany, United Arab Emirates, India, and Singapore for large Western multinational corporations. He explains: "I interact with people from around the world on a daily basis. The global perspective I gained through regular travel along with multiple overseas assignments enables me to both relate and adapt to my clients and team members through demonstrating my understanding of their respective cultural backgrounds."[13]

The current generation of senior Chinese management may unintentionally view their global business through a "Chinese lens" due to limited exposure to cultures and business practices outside China. This is changing rapidly, however, as an increasing number of Chinese executives are studying at international executive MBA programs both within and outside of China. In an interview with *The New York Times*, Qian Yingyi, Dean of the School of Economics and Management at Beijing's prestigious Tsinghua University, explains: "The average age of our executive MBA students is 41 or 42, with almost 20 years work experience – they are much older than their counterparts in Europe or the US." He attributes the rise in interest in obtaining a global business education to the fact that Chinese executives "simply didn't have a chance to study global business in their 20's."[14] As dramatic economic and political changes swept China during the reform and opening period, they spent the early years of their careers building their companies at home.

Related to an individual's level of internationalization are his or her foreign language abilities. The most seasoned Chinese executive may come across as a novice with limited language skills. Mastery of a foreign language is much less a challenge for Western companies entering China, where English is almost always the working language at multinational firms. English is a required subject in China's high schools and universities, so there are typically sufficient English speakers for Western executives to communicate with, thereby enabling them to work relatively unaffected by language barriers. Successful executives from Western companies can live in a city like Beijing or Shanghai for over 20 years and never need to learn a word of Chinese. However, this is not the case for Chinese corporate leaders working overseas. The boom in Chinese outbound tourism and international MBA education occurring today will boost the English skills and internationalization of future Chinese executives. However, for now many senior executives, especially those from state-owned firms, still lack the global experience and language ability requisite for overseas management success.

Differences in management style

Chinese executives may also be accustomed to managing their teams differently from Western managers. Dr. Wei explains the challenges she faced when first joining Lenovo as a full-time employee. At the time Dr. Wei had two bosses: she reported to an American executive in the US and also to a Chinese executive in Beijing. "My American boss always expected me to express my opinion and offer suggestions. If I didn't agree with something she said, I could openly share my view." Dr. Wei had grown accustomed to direct feedback while interacting with peers and professors during her studies at Harvard. However, her Chinese manager had very different expectations.

Given the traditionally hierarchical culture within Chinese firms, some Chinese managers may take direct feedback or differences of opinion as a challenge to their authority. For that reason, Qian Yingyi of Tsinghua University's School of Economics and Management notes, in general Chinese employees "just don't like to give such honest evaluations – they are afraid that others will take things too personally." At Lenovo, Dr. Wei spent time building an understanding with her Chinese boss that by sharing her own opinion, she did not intend to undermine her boss's authority. Eventually, Dr. Wei was able to interact in a similar way with both of her bosses. However, it is unlikely that the majority of Chinese managers operating in the global business environment for the first time are able to have such open conversations with their employees in order to overcome cultural differences. According to Qian Yingyi of Tsinghua University, Chinese managers tend to lack the "softer" skills of management, which he defines as "things like teamwork, communications, presentations, culture – all the skills that help you deal with people."[15] Unless both sides invest time in learning about each other's cultures and values, distrust and conflicts between team members will be difficult to avoid.

Differences in decision-making

Matthew Clearfield, Managing Director at private equity firm Elaixin Holdings, recounts the story of a Chinese friend who worked with a state-owned Chinese company in Beijing and took time off to earn an MBA in the US. After completing the MBA and welcoming a first child, his friend planned to work for a Western investment bank in Shanghai. Matthew could not understand why his friend was willing to give up his stable "iron rice bowl" job at the SOE for years of long hours at an investment bank. His friend replied: "It's simple. The rules in a state-owned Chinese company are very straightforward – you're not able to make any decisions until you are in your 40's or 50's. Until then the basic rule is 'don't make any mistakes.'" But the only way not to make any mistakes, he said, is to not make any decisions. "I don't want to spend the next 20 years of my life not making any decisions."[16]

This view is shared by many employees of private and hybrid as well as state-owned Chinese companies. According to Dr. Wei: "Generally speaking, Chinese employees are most comfortable being told what to do and are relatively risk averse." It's not that they are not willing to take risks, it's that they worry about disrupting the harmony between them and their superiors by doing so. A wrong decision could lead to strained relations and even major career setbacks. As Michael Crain, Beijing-based senior consultant for global law firm Bingham McCutchen, explains: "If a Chinese general manager recommends that the company acquire an overseas firm, his or her career might be over if the deal goes bad. Conversely, if that same general manager does not mention anything about the potential acquisition target, then no one back at headquarters would have the knowledge to hold him or her accountable for the missed opportunity."[17]

Adding to this difficulty is the fact that Chinese managers leading their firm's operations in the West often lack the ability to make business decisions without approval from corporate headquarters in China. For any company in the early stages of operating abroad, a balance must be found between centralized decision-making at headquarters in the home country, and decentralized decision-making in the overseas offices. If overseas offices have little autonomy, then Chinese managers on the ground will constantly have to verify decisions with their bosses in China – sometimes waiting up to 12 hours to do so given time differences. This lesser degree of autonomy slows decision-making and leads to missed opportunities, especially in a dynamic global business environment which rewards quick thinking and decisiveness.

Relationship 3: company to customers

Depending on its business model and the nature of a given industry, a company's relationship with its customers may vary widely. People typically think of "customers" as the individual consumers who purchase products from companies. Companies that serve "consumers" have a business-to-consumer (B2C) model, like sports apparel company Li-Ning or beverage maker Jianlibao. Alternatively, if a company sells products or services to another company, it uses a business-to-business (B2B) model, like wind power firm Goldwind or industrial manufacturer Zoomlion. B2B businesses tend to be less consumer facing and may only be recognized by the specific companies that operate in their industry (Table 3.2).

Table 3.2   Examples of Chinese B2C companies vs B2B companies

Business-to-consumer (B2C)	Business-to-business (B2B)
Li-Ning (*Athletic apparel*)	Wanxiang (*Automotive*)
Jianlibao (*Beverages*)	Huawei (*Telecommunications*)
Lenovo (*Consumer electronics*)	Goldwind (*Wind energy*)
Tencent (*Online services*)	Sany Heavy (*Industrials*)
Haier (*Home appliances*)	ChemChina (*Chemicals*)

Business-to-consumer (B2C)

In its unsuccessful initial attempt to enter the US market, Li-Ning did not understand American consumers. It did not adequately understand their likes and dislikes, and it did very little initial research into American consumer behavior. Companies in the B2C space often face extremely high levels of competition in the US and other developed markets. They will need to build their brand through years of experience and millions of dollars of investment and marketing to convince Western consumers of the value they have to offer. This may be especially challenging for Chinese firms because of the longstanding perception among Western consumers that Chinese-produced goods are cheap and poor quality. Chapter 4 covers Chinese firms' ability to build globally recognized brands in more depth.

Alternatively, Chinese firms can choose to appeal to overseas consumers in developed and emerging markets based purely on the simple "price-value equation." In other words, if the price is significantly cheaper than the existing product on the market, and the quality of the Chinese product is 90 percent as good, or it has 90 percent of the features, then the Chinese product can be successful in meeting the needs of consumers overseas. This is the approach consumer-facing Chinese firms often take when entering emerging markets. According to Joel Whitaker, Senior Vice President of Global Research for Frontier Strategy Group: "Western multinational executives in the consumer sector rank Chinese competition among their top challenges in emerging markets. They find that Chinese competitors are very successful adapting existing products originally intended for Chinese shoppers to the needs of consumers in markets across South East Asia and Sub-Saharan Africa. They offer an attractive price for a decent product."[18] However, if Chinese firms in the B2C space want to build brands able to compete with the likes of Coca-Cola and Nike, then they will have to develop capabilities to compete in the premium segment, going head-to-head with market leaders and winning as a result of having more innovative products that fulfill a need consumers can't otherwise satisfy with existing products from Western competitors.

Business-to-business (B2B)

Chinese firms in the B2B space may have a slightly easier time appealing to their customers overseas. Potentially they can build on existing relationships in China with current Western customers. For example, if Wanxiang designs and supplies a component for a General Motors (GM) automobile produced in China, on day one of its expansion in the US Wanxiang can potentially expand its existing relationship by approaching GM in the US rather than starting with zero customers or prospects. Chinese companies in the B2B space will have to assuage the following concerns when beginning new customer relationships overseas. Questions they are likely to face include: *"Will the Chinese company pay on time?"* *"Will they share our company information with competitors?"* *"Will they honor our contract?"* All of these questions are valid concerns for overseas customers doing business with unfamiliar Chinese firms.

While Western firms have a long history of relying on highly formalized legal contracts to mitigate the risks associated with building new customer relationships in the B2B space, Chinese firms are still learning. Yuan Haiying, President of government relations consulting firm Yuan Associates, explains: "If you look at Chinese history, it's a *shuren shehui* (熟人社会) or a 'familiar people society.' It's vital to know whom you are doing business with." This is in contrast to the West, which is a contractual society with a long history of formalized, impersonal relationships based on legal obligation: "I have a contract with you, I don't need to be friends with you." There is not as much value in contracts when you live in a *shuren shehui*. Interpersonal connections work to prevent wrongdoings, to keep people honest, and to ensure they fulfill their obligations – at least in theory. As Yuan explains: "When you take a Chinese firm that's coming from a *shuren shehui*, and they go abroad where they don't know anyone, then they don't trust anyone. Chinese firms only trust people who they know, and who they know well."[19]

However, the expanding scale of modern markets means that China is moving quickly from a "know everyone society" to a "know no one society."

In this context, formal legal contracts are becoming more and more important. "But many Chinese firms still don't pay attention to contracts when they do business. They don't honor contracts," says Yuan. When a Chinese company fails to honor its contractual commitments with a Western partner and informal relations sour, it generates mistrust on both sides. "The real question is – how can we build a contractual society in China? That's the key challenge," says Dan Harris, a partner at international law firm HarrisMoure and author of the China Law Blog. He explains that Chinese companies entering developed markets like the US for the first time often do not understand how to effectively manage customer relationships in the West. "There is an enduring lack of trust toward Chinese companies investing in the US. The perception is that Chinese firms do not understand the importance of the legally binding contracts with their American partners. As Chinese firms increase their presence in international markets, it is critical that they embrace contractual business practices more fully."[20]

Relationship 4: company to community

Any company entering a new market must be prepared for how it will be perceived by the local community and adopt a strategy for managing local relations. Companies with experience operating abroad will frequently invest in Corporate Social Responsibility (CSR) programs, sponsor charitable events, and engage in a variety of initiatives to demonstrate that the firm is out to improve the domestic economy – and community – in addition to making money. Community engagement also makes overseas firms seem "less foreign" and therefore less prone to provoke public outcry against their operations. This is especially important in industries like natural resources or agriculture, where domestic publics may be particularly sensitive to foreign investment or presence. Ideally, firms should adopt a preemptive rather than a reactive strategy to ensure their business is welcomed – or at least tolerated – by local communities overseas.

Chinese companies are facing a "perception gap" in the West between how they want to be viewed and how the West views them. "Chinese firms want to be viewed as sophisticated, savvy buyers of companies in advanced global economies, capable of managing and operating them profitably, safeguarding jobs and capitalizing on the technological advancements or market opportunities presented with such acquisitions," explains John Kao, Partner-in-Charge of global law firm Jones Day's Beijing Office.[21] But for many industry insiders in the merger and acquisition (M&A) space, there is instead a general perception that Chinese businesses expanding overseas are in fact unsophisticated buyers of poor-performing Western firms.

For general publics in Western nations, perceptions of Chinese firms are often not much better. Unfortunately, many in the West view Chinese firms with suspicion due to politicization of their investments by Western officials and media and highly visible scandals related to "made-in-China" goods. Rather than learn about the 3,000 American jobs created by Wanxiang over the past two decades, the Western media tend to focus on the controversial side of Chinese investment overseas. Telecommunications firm Huawei Technologies made headlines in the US, Australia, and UK over concerns about potential security threats posed by its telecommunications systems. When Shuanghui International announced its takeover of American pork processor Smithfield Foods in May 2013, it evoked a massive public outcry about food security concerns. Just a few months earlier, Shanghai had made international news as thousands of dead pigs mysteriously floated down the Huangpu River. After decades of news stories highlighting Chinese firms' missteps at home and abroad, the West is wary of Chinese firms operating in their own backyard. Chapter 6 discusses the concerns associated with Chinese investment in the West in greater detail, while Chapter 8 provides guidance to Chinese firms about how they can overcome this "perception gap" when expanding overseas.

Relationship 5: company to capital

The last and perhaps most fundamental relationship is *company to capital*. Without sufficient funding, even the best-laid overseas expansion plans will not reach fruition. Investing enough money into overseas offices, paying employees competitive incentive packages, and further investing in the growth of the business are all critical factors in overseas expansion. As the next chapter explains, Chinese companies that want to build globally recognized brands from the ground up have no choice but to invest hundreds of millions of dollars into marketing and brand-building initiatives. Global brands are a long-term investment and require significant capital investment over the course of a multi-year strategy. Short-term investment tied to the latest product release will not enable a Chinese firm to achieve global brand recognition.

Key takeaways from this chapter

The central argument from Chapter 3 is that the majority of Chinese companies are not yet fully ready to go West. They are currently experiencing a natural transition, "paying their tuition" through first-hand experience; learning from their own and other's missteps to ultimately become more globally competitive.

By mastering each of the five relationships from this chapter – (i) company to government, (ii) company to employees, (iii) company to customers, (iv) company to community, and (v) company to capital – Chinese firms will be able to compete more effectively overseas. Lenovo's success creating a global multinational company serves as an example for other Chinese firms that it is possible to effectively manage the five key relationships. However, more success stories for Chinese companies to study are needed to build more globally competitive Chinese firms. But how Chinese firms will be perceived in the West is also tied to how they manage their brands and reputations. This is the central question of Chapter 4: *Do Chinese firms have what it takes to build global brands?*

Part II

The Approach

4

Global Recognition: Can Chinese Firms Build Global Brands?

Three years after Li Jingwei, founder of Jianlibao Group, met Li Ning following the 1988 Seoul Olympic Games, he began to plan his own firm's United States expansion. Jianlibao was the number one consumer beverage in China at the time. Its sweet honey taste with light carbonation offered a differentiated product which had enabled it to compete with major players such as Coca-Cola and Pepsi in its home market. But leading the market in China alone was not enough for Li Jingwei. He dreamed of transforming Jianlibao into a truly global brand like Coke: a brand that transcends borders yet still appeals to consumers' local tastes. With such a global brand, consumers would not question where the beverage originated. It would not be "China's Jianlibao." It would be "Jianlibao, a delicious beverage brand enjoyed by consumers around the world, enriching lives one can at a time."

Yet Li's dream would not be achieved easily. In his first attempt to build a global brand, in 1991 Li invested five million dollars in office space in New York City's Empire State Building.[1] He held a major press conference at the office opening with the New York City mayor in attendance praising Chinese investment in the city. Like many Chinese companies, Li placed too much emphasis on the role that government, political connections, and prestige plays in facilitating business in the West. Unfortunately, two years later Jianlibao was far from a mainstream brand in the US. In 1994, Jianlibao finally hired an executive with expertise in the American market to help build the brand. Jack Shea, an American food and beverage industry veteran, assumed the role of vice-president of marketing and sales for North America. According to Shea: "Jianlibao's fatal error was that while it produced a good-tasting beverage, its Chinese brand name prevented it from being able to connect with the average American consumer."[2]

Beyond branding issues, Shea found that after three years of investment in the US market, Jianlibao USA's capital was beginning to dry up. Shea recalled: "Our North America operations did not have a sufficient marketing budget to make the necessary investments to promote Jianlibao within the United States." Even if an American consumer wanted to try Jianlibao, the company didn't have effective distribution channels to get its drink on store shelves across the country. Ironically, at the same time its US operations were faltering, Jianlibao hit a new peak in the Chinese market with 5 billion *renminbi* in revenues in 1997. But its US operations soon proved a costly distraction from its market leadership in China. One year later, Pepsi and Coca-Cola combined took 50 percent market share of China's soft drink market. Jianlibao was hit the hardest in Beijing and Guangzhou, two of China's largest cities, where in 1998 it witnessed its share of the soft drink market shrink to single digits.

Similar to Li-Ning's experience, after investing millions of dollars in the US market, Jianlibao ultimately closed down its American operations a few years later and retreated to China to defend its brand against Pepsi, Coca-Cola, and local competitors. Jianlibao went overseas too early. Rather than shore up its dominant position in China first, Li Jingwei's global aspirations distracted the firm from focusing on the larger market where it had a strong initial competitive advantage.[3] Without prior experience of operating outside of China, Jianlibao failed to understand where to invest its money to successfully build its brand in the American market. It spent too much money on winning politicians' recognition and making high profile real estate investments, and not enough on marketing or building local expertise to drive short-term sales and establish its brand in the US market for the long term. Chinese companies have a lot to learn when it comes to building successful global brands.

Chinese companies are still catching up

Chapter 1 discusses how Chinese companies have significantly fewer years of business operating experience compared with their industry peers from the West. Chapter 3 explains that, as a result of their relative youth, Chinese companies are only now actively learning from their mistakes and triumphs, just as American and European firms did previously in history. These two truths about Chinese overseas investment are extremely relevant to the topic of Chinese firms' branding overseas. Chinese companies are learning how to brand effectively in China and abroad at the same time. The historic lack of focus on marketing as a core function within many Chinese companies requires an increased emphasis on global brand strategy. Marketing needs to play a central role in international expansion – from product development, to product localization and overseas pricing strategy. If marketing is an afterthought, even the best-laid plans won't work. Not every firm's overseas brand expansion faces the same disastrous fate as Li Jingwei's Jianlibao did in the American market, but the overall sentiment among global marketers is that China's current ability to build global brands is bleak.

That said, the challenges Chinese firms face in building brands overseas are not insurmountable. This chapter begins with an analysis of the characteristics of a global brand, identifies what challenges Chinese companies currently face, and offers perspectives on how Chinese firms can better build globally recognizable brands.

> The challenges Chinese firms face in building brands overseas are not insurmountable.

Defining a "global brand"

What is a "global brand"? Tom Doctoroff, CEO of Asia Pacific for advertising firm J. Walter Thompson (JWT), explains: "A global brand is a brand that is able to compete at a price premium in developed markets."[4] In other words, the brand itself holds intrinsic value beyond the cost associated with the product. Therefore, consumers will be willing to pay a higher price for a branded product when faced with a decision between similar options. Scott Bedbury, former head of marketing for Starbucks and Nike, elaborates: "If you take a long-term approach, a great brand can travel worldwide, transcend cultural barriers, speak to multiple consumer segments simultaneously, create economies of scale, and let you operate at the higher end of the positioning spectrum – where you can earn solid margins over the long term."[5]

Five common views about why Chinese brands fall short

Any article about China's ability to build global brands typically begins in a very similar fashion. It starts by asking the reader: "How many Chinese brands can you name?" The journalist expects most people to think to themselves: "None, except maybe Lenovo and Huawei." Then the article quotes a brand perception study conducted by a well-respected multinational advertising firm. "According to a recent brand awareness study conducted by a reputable Western advertising firm, not a single Chinese company appeared on its list." This type of introduction is meant to prepare readers to learn about the reasons why there are no well-known Chinese brands in their country, and why they are not coming anytime soon.

Industry experts working with Chinese firms express multiple commonly held views about why, generally speaking, Chinese companies have been unsuccessful in their efforts to build global brands thus far. Based on a series of conversations with some of the top minds in China in branding

Table 4.1   Five common views about why Chinese brands fall short

i. Chinese firms see marketing & branding as an expendable expense
ii. Chinese firms do not believe marketing is a strategic activity
iii. Chinese leadership is unwilling to solicit ideas from the outside
iv. Chinese firms are too shortsighted
v. Chinese business culture focuses on compliance, not striking first

and marketing, five common views about why Chinese brands fall short can be identified (Table 4.1). These views link back to the characteristics of a global brand introduced above. The following section examines each of them in detail.

View 1: Chinese firms see marketing and branding as an expendable expense

David Wolf, managing director of the Global China Practice at public relations consultancy Allison+Partners, once referred to a common joke among China business observers: "For most [state-owned enterprises], 'branding' means getting a new logo, 'marketing' means buying ads on China Central Television, and 'P.R.' stands for 'pay the reporter'."[6] While this statement is somewhat exaggerated, it does illustrate the perceived general lack of emphasis by Chinese firms of brand importance and how a company's marketing efforts can build it over time.

In a separate interview for this book, Wolf explained how the intangible nature of a brand makes it more difficult for Chinese corporate leaders to view it as a central operation and not as an expendable function. For over three decades, China's economic growth was the result of serving as the world's factory. As Chinese companies flooded overseas markets with inexpensive goods, their owners developed the mentality: "This is what I make, now who will buy it?" As the competitive landscape has evolved, the question they should be asking instead is: "What does the market want and how can I produce a differentiated product to fulfill demand?" Many firms have failed to make this transition in their attitude toward brand building and the investment needed to achieve it.[7]

View 2: Chinese firms do not believe marketing is a strategic activity

Tom Doctoroff of JWT notes: "In any organization, the responsibility of marketing is to balance long-term brand equity building with short-term sales." Sales teams, by their nature, are almost exclusively focused on short-term results. Therefore, unless a firm has an empowered marketing department vis-à-vis its sales team, it is very difficult to strike a balance between sales promotion and brand-building activities. Doctoroff elaborates: "I know of very few Chinese companies – in fact none – that have a marketing department at the center of international expansion and which is charged with leading product development, adapting products for local tastes, and adjusting pricing strategy to penetrate local markets."

The perception remains that for many Chinese companies, even very large firms, marketing is not a priority function in the organization. Such firms take a highly instrumental approach to marketing, focusing on short-term product launches and advertising initiatives. In contrast, companies that succeed in establishing brand reputations for product quality invest in building their long-term strategic marketing functions. A central part of their global marketing function is having the right internationally experienced talent. "Make no mistake, you cannot have successful brands without marketing expertise that is internationalized in its perspective," warns Doctoroff.[8]

View 3: leadership is unwilling to solicit ideas from the outside

"In general, Chinese companies do not understand how to incorporate feedback from their customers and seek advice from external advisors to build great brands," says Justin Knapp, who heads Ogilvy Public Relations' China Outbound Practice. Customer insight and advice from marketing and branding agencies make a world of difference when trying to build a brand in a new market for the first time. Companies need always to be listening to their customers for ways to improve their products and brand positioning, and then adapting accordingly. As Knapp emphasizes: "A brand isn't successful until the local market says so."[9]

Personal electronics firm Apple does an excellent job of incorporating feedback from customers to design and market products in a way that is targeted to their needs. It does not simply go to its consumers with the usual message from most companies of "we made a great computer, would you like to buy one?" Author and innovation expert, Simon Sinek describes how Apple instead communicates what it stands for, rather than simply talking about what it produces. He explains Apple's brand positioning: "Everything we do, we believe in challenging the status quo. We believe in thinking differently. The way we challenge the status quo is by making our products beautifully designed, simple to use and user friendly. We just happened to make great computers. Want to buy one?" That's a much more compelling message for consumers.[10]

In addition, Chinese firms often have little appetite for seeking advice from third parties about intangible knowledge-based services like marketing, branding or public relations. Bill Black, who leads the Global China Practice at public relations firm Fleishman Hillard, notes: "When I ask potential Chinese clients about the first thing they would do if they were to expand their business from Beijing to Guangdong, they reply 'find someone I trust on the ground to help me navigate the local business environment.' Given this, it is remarkable there is such reluctance to trust Western professional services firms to help build locally relevant brands for customers in the West."[11] To create global brands, Chinese firms will have to place more trust in local partners with experience in, and understanding of, overseas markets.

View 4: Chinese firms are too shortsighted

Scott Markman, President of The Monogram Group, a Chicago-based brand advisory firm focused on serving Chinese companies, observes: "In general, the Chinese companies I work with struggle with corporate branding – it is too abstract for them to be willing to make it a strategic priority. They are most comfortable with the today and the tangible – the ring of the cash register."[12] Markman is not the only one who feels this way. Doctoroff adds: "The challenge is an underlying attitude of 'short-termism', and by this I mean a focus on short-term sales." As a result, there is often too much impatience and overemphasis on making quick sales in order to justify the "risk" associated with expanding in international markets.

This perceived short-term mindset links brand success to short-term product performance, rather than to long-term strategy. Many Chinese firms' business culture has not yet evolved to a point where there is clear understanding and acceptance that long-term brand strategy and identity sit apart from the firm's latest product or latest advertising campaign. There needs to be an acknowledgement that brand building is a far more long-term commitment, and one that is worth making. "There is so much emphasis on delivery – let's get that product out – and there is so little sense of 'we're the brand that believes X' who we are and how we should communicate. So all the company ends up doing is focusing on the products," says Doctoroff.[13] The planning and investment that are needed to realize a long-term brand vision all too often get swept aside amid focus on short-term firm performance.

View 5: culture of compliance, not striking first

This fifth perception alludes to the need for a company to be prepared to fail multiple times in the process of creating a great global brand. Ed Booty is the former Director of International Planning at Bartle Bogle Hegarty (BBH) Group, where he worked with Chinese firms including Huawei on their global advertising accounts. "What is fascinating about the Chinese firms I have encountered is the Confucian notion of all corporate decision-makers heading in the same direction – reflecting a respect for scale and consensus. Many of these companies are looking more for a model to replicate rather than forging their own paths."[14] The popular Chinese saying *qiang da chutou niao* (枪打出头鸟) aptly illustrates Chinese firms' attitude toward risk taking. They do not want to take the first risk, because "the bird leading the flock is the first to be shot." While many Chinese companies have made innovation an official corporate objective, few demonstrate their commitment to this ideal in their strategic practices. Instead, they prefer to follow rather than lead. They simply do not want to go beyond their comfort zone. However, categorical risk aversion will hinder Chinese companies from building global brands in the short term.

These five views are commonly held among members of the global marketing community about the key factors holding Chinese companies back from building global brands. Yet none of these views and challenges is insurmountable for Chinese firms in the long term. The following sections look at next steps to show how Chinese companies could construct – and in some cases are already building – global brands.

Three paths for Chinese firms to build global brands

Chinese firms have several different strategic options when it comes to building globally recognized brands. They can identify an existing global brand and buy it; they can build a respected niche brand; or they can create globally recognized brand names themselves. Each of these three potential paths has its own advantages and challenges (Table 4.2).

Path 1: buy an existing global brand

Tong Zhicheng wanted Pearl River Piano to become a famous piano brand in the West. After working for the Guangzhou-based firm since 1958, he became the company's president in 1992. At that time, Pearl River pianos dominated the Chinese market. However, the Chinese piano market was relatively small, and Pearl River Piano faced increasing competition from emerging Chinese firms. Tong dedicated his efforts to improving the quality of Pearl River's pianos in order to create new markets in the United States and Europe. Tong told industry insiders: "Pianos are from the West. Success in Western markets is the only thing that can prove the high quality of our pianos."[15]

Table 4.2　Three paths for Chinese firms to build global brands

1. Buy an existing global brand
2. Build a respected niche brand
3. Create a globally recognized brand through own investment and efforts

Through a series of strategic moves, including a joint venture with Japanese piano maker Yamaha, Tong quickly improved the quality of Pearl River's pianos and the efficiency of its production processes. The Yamaha joint venture enabled Pearl River Piano to access advanced technology and establish a localized presence in the US. As Pearl River continued to expand its overseas presence and capabilities, Tong realized that something was missing from his strategy. A piano is not a highly price-sensitive purchase, given that most consumers may only buy one piano over the course of their lifetimes. Therefore, selling pianos overseas by competing on price alone would cheapen Pearl River's pianos in the eyes of Western consumers. Tong needed to find an existing brand with a long history of excellence in the premium piano market.

Tong discovered the perfect addition to the Pearl River Piano portfolio in Germany. In 1999, he acquired the brand license and technology to produce Germany's Ritmüller pianos. The Ritmüller Piano Company, established in 1795, was one of Europe's most famous traditional piano companies. Not only did Tong purchase the Ritmüller brand, he also hired international master piano designer Lothar Thomma to refine the designs using the latest piano manufacturing technology. The Ritmüller brand license acquisition gave Pearl River the premium brand it needed to increase its competitiveness in the West. By 2006, these strategic acquisitions ultimately enabled Tong to achieve his dream of Pearl River Piano becoming the world's largest piano manufacturer.

Pearl River's acquisition of the Ritmüller brand was a crucial move in its overseas expansion, not only because it boosted the firm's reputation in the premium market, but also because it opened new markets outside China for both Ritmüller and Pearl River branded pianos. European and American consumers had long known of Ritmüller's reputation for producing excellent high-end pianos. Pearl River's further investment in improving their traditional designs with modern technology showed piano enthusiasts that Pearl River's own branded pianos were worth trying as well. Ritmüller gave Pearl River a brand in its product portfolio that consumers associated with a long-established history of quality German precision craftsmanship. At the same time, as consumers familiarized themselves with Pearl River pianos marketed alongside Ritmüller, they began also to develop a positive association with the Chinese brand name.[16]

Branding has always played a key role in Pearl River's success overseas. Not all Chinese brands have the luxury of owning a brand name like "Pearl River" that is easily intelligible and pronounceable by a Western audience. Western consumers find trying to pronounce brand names like "Wanxiang," "Haier," "Huawei," and "Tsingtao" more challenging than some childhood tongue twisters. How can a Western audience relate to a brand whose name they cannot even pronounce correctly? Brand acquisitions of established Western firms can also help to bridge this gap. The Chinese firm can then operate under the acquired firm's name, rather than teach Westerners how to pronounce Chinese. Following TCL's acquisition of American electronics firm RCA, Vincent Yan, Chief Financial Officer for TCL explained: "Our strategy is to utilize the RCA name globally. To build a brand in a mature market is costly, we don't plan to do that."[17] Other examples of this strategy include Dalian Wanda's decision to keep the AMC brand name, and Shuanghui International's choice to do the same following its acquisition of Smithfield Foods.

Bright Food's acquisition of New Zealand's Synliat Milk, discussed in Chapter 2, also illustrates the important role a respected international brand can play in earning customer trust. By acquiring Synliat Milk, Bright Food was able to begin to regain consumers' trust in China's domestic market after the 2008 dairy product safety scandal. Chapter 5 examines Bright Food's high profile acquisition of UK breakfast cereal Weetabix to shed light on how Chinese investment can benefit long-standing Western brands facing tough times due to slowing growth in developed economies.

Path 2: build a global brand in a niche industry

When Wu Gang, founder of wind power producer Goldwind, led the firm into the North American market in 2010, he was careful to learn from the mistakes of other Chinese companies before him. Rather than appoint a fully Chinese management team, he hired American and Canadian industry veterans from global energy firms including First Wind, Gamesa, Enel, and GE Energy. In addition to hiring skilled global leadership, Wu gave the management team autonomy to run the Americas operations, all the way from Toronto, Canada to Chicago, USA to Santiago, Chile. Part of this autonomy meant that the Americas team could work with local experts to build a Goldwind brand relevant for its North and South American customers. To redefine the Goldwind brand for an American audience, Goldwind's management team turned to The Monogram Group, a Chicago-based brand consultancy. Monogram worked with Goldwind USA's marketing team, led by Nancy Cook, Director of Marketing and Strategy. Cook explains: "The Chinese management's support for the Americas business to build the Goldwind USA brand has been critical to its success. As a business-to-business firm, Goldwind may not be a household name among consumers, but it has become an established brand leader in the international wind energy space."[18]

A misconception about Chinese brands "going West" is that they must appeal to the mass market in order to be successful. Goldwind is an example of a Chinese firm that is not a household name, but is a recognized brand leader in its industry. Goldwind's ability to brand itself for its target audience of potential customers has allowed it to earn trust within the wind power industry based on the firm's technology, experience, and expertise. Like Goldwind, multiple other Chinese firms have created global brands by focusing their marketing efforts to develop reputations within their industry. For example, while "Wanxiang" may be an unfamiliar name to many in the West, this new energy and automotive supplier firm is already a global industry brand leader with operations in North America, the EU, and Australia.

Although global industry brand leadership tends to be claimed by less consumer-facing Chinese companies operating in the business-to-business (B2B) space, there are also Chinese consumer goods brands that have not achieved mass-market success but are well-known brands in their respective areas. For instance, Haier produces a wide range of products that may not all be familiar to mass consumers, but it is unmatched when it comes to refrigerators. Since 2008, Haier has been the world's largest producer of refrigerators, surpassing Western giants like General Electric, Whirlpool, and Electrolux.[19] Despite high-profile branding attempts – like sponsoring the National Basketball Association (NBA) or taking a page out of Jianlibao's book and investing in the Haier Building in New York City – Haier remains far from a mass-market global brand in the West. However, executives at every single one of the Western competitors listed above surely know the Haier brand and are strategizing every day to take back market leadership from the Chinese consumer electronics and home appliances firm.

> A misconception about Chinese brands "going West" is that they must appeal to the mass market in order to be successful.

Path 3: build a well-known Chinese-owned global brand

The third path Chinese firms can choose is to build a widely recognized global brand from the ground up through years of long-term investment and management commitment. To expedite the global brand-building process, Chinese firms should apply a strategy developed by one of China's most prominent authors. Lu Xun, a major Chinese writer of the early 1900s, is considered one of the foremost figures in modern Chinese literary history. He coined the phrase *nalaizhuyi* (拿来主义), which refers to a philosophy of taking the best parts from a variety of sources to create something that is even better. When applied to global branding, Lu Xun's theory boils down to combining global innovation practices, marketing methods, and international talent to create a brand which consumers around the world will recognize. To accomplish this, Chinese firms will need to hire senior marketing leadership from the West; partner with global advertising, marketing, and public relations firms; and incorporate ideas from their customers. While there has yet to be a Chinese brand that consumers around the world unanimously recognize, Chinese companies can look at past experiences from their Asian neighbors in Japan and Korea to see how many of their firms adopted a *"nalaizhuyi* approach" to global brand leadership.

Both Japanese and Korean firms were viewed with skepticism and even suspicion when they first went West. Their products were thought to be cheap and inferior, and their management teams were characterized as being highly inward facing and lacking the necessary global know-how to build global brands. Over time, both nations' companies began investing in product design, with an eye toward cultural sensitivity, and in brand and perception building. Samsung is an excellent example of a traditional Korean *chaebol*, or conglomerate, that has reinvented itself over the course of the last two decades. Samsung originally sold cheap television sets in low-cost retail outlets like Wal-Mart and Carrefour. By the mid-1990s, it was losing money and the Asian financial crisis only deepened its financial woes. But instead of going bankrupt, Samsung repositioned itself as a premium market brand by focusing on product innovation, investing heavily in marketing, and hiring global talent from the outside to internationalize its business practices.[20] The Samsung brand has become one of the most widely recognized in the world. There is no reason why a Chinese company cannot adopt a *nalaizhuyi* approach to take the best elements of each aspect of building a global brand and similarly transform how its own business is viewed.

New business dynamics herald the rise of Chinese global brands

As China's business environment continues to evolve, two shifting dynamics herald the rise of Chinese global brands: climbing business costs at home in the short term and the rise of a new generation of global consumers in the long term. Both trends require a shift at many Chinese companies from brand development being a "nice to have" to becoming a recognized "need to have" component of their global strategy.

Moving up the value chain

Chinese firms are in the process of adapting to a changing operating environment in which they cannot survive simply by competing to be the cheapest option. Global brand equity, the international reputation gained from building brands overseas, allows companies to charge more by differentiating themselves from competitors. This is a key element of the strategy Chinese firms need to adopt to remain competitive in the next decade. In *The End of Cheap China*, Shaun Rein writes: "Chinese brands are quickly moving up the value chain to compete on branding and innovation rather than just on price ... Rising labor and real estate costs and demanding consumers are forcing them to think more long term about building sustainable brands and changing manufacturing operations, in order to command the fatter margins they need to stay alive."[21] An increased focus on branding and product innovation through investment in research and development will be vital for Chinese firms to differentiate themselves from domestic competitors in the short term. During this process, they will learn to adapt their marketing approaches to target the variety of consumer segments they will again encounter when expanding overseas.

A generational shift

Over the long term, the greater cosmopolitanism of young consumers in China may help boost Chinese companies seeking to build world-class brands. While few Chinese global brands exist today, it would be foolish to suggest that the Chinese branding landscape of today will be that of tomorrow. Chinese youth and their parents are traveling overseas in record numbers and Chinese consumers are interacting with companies from around the world in their living room on a daily basis through mobile devices. At the same time, greater numbers of *haigui* managers are returning to teach and implement global business practices. "This generation of Chinese citizens is more exposed to global brands than any other in history," says Julia Q. Zhu, Founder and Managing Director of China e-commerce research firm Observer Solutions.[22] Zhu points to the example of WeChat, a branded group-messaging mobile application produced by Chinese Internet giant Tencent. "WeChat is unique since very early on in its development, a significant percentage of users came from outside of China. The bulk of users are part of this new generation of young globally minded consumers between the ages of 20 and 30." The generational shift, both at the corporate leadership level and global consumer level will be critical to overcome the majority of obstacles Chinese firms currently face in building global brands.

> Over the long term, the greater cosmopolitanism of young consumers in China may help boost Chinese companies seeking to build world-class brands.

According to David Roman, Chief Marketing Officer at Lenovo:

> For the time being, many big companies with roots in China and other emerging markets are invisible to global consumers. However, the business success – brand momentum gap – and the time it has historically taken to grow a global brand may be providing a false sense of security to some well-established brands in the West. As emerging market companies leverage their home court advantage and discover ways to appeal to the [millennial generation], top global brands should pay careful attention to the shifting competitive landscape.[23]

It will take time for a new generation of globally minded consumers to begin shopping for Chinese brands. For now Chinese managers can move to build global brands by bringing Western managers into their organizations. However, long-term success may require Chinese global managers at the helm who are capable of working across cultures and geographies to build internationally competitive brands.

Key takeaways from this chapter

The central argument of this chapter is that Chinese companies can build global brands – but most have not done so yet. Although global marketing leaders currently may share the view that Chinese firms cannot build global brands, the fact is that firms simply take time to develop and adapt.

Multiple possible paths exist for Chinese firms to build global brands: acquiring existing brands, growing their own industry-specific global brand, or building a mass-market Chinese-owned global brand. The most successful Chinese brands will be the ones capable of going beyond their country of origin and positioning themselves as "global brands" rather than "Chinese global brands." This is not going to happen tomorrow – it may not occur for decades – but when you look at all the components of building a global brand, none is insurmountable for Chinese companies. It will take time, investment, the right leadership, and examples of successful (and unsuccessful) companies to pave the way.

5

China's Overseas M&A Moment: Buying Up the World's Corporations?

"We were like a poor farm boy pursuing a famous movie star," said Li Shufu, Chairman of Chinese automaker Geely. Li was comparing Sweden's Volvo to a famous movie star being pursued by his lesser-known Chinese firm, Geely, during its 2010 acquisition. But Li was not always a prominent business figure in the global automobile industry. He began his entrepreneurial endeavors in 1982 at age 19 when he bought a camera with his high school graduation money and began a small-scale photography business, taking photos of tourists for a modest fee. This operation later evolved into a photography studio where he also sold handmade camera accessories. His real-world "postgraduate studies" in entrepreneurship continued in 1984 when he invested his earnings from the photography business to open a refrigerator parts company. At first he produced parts for other factories, but eventually he founded his own refrigerator company.

In 1993, on a visit to a state-owned motorcycle factory, Li saw a new opportunity. With the expertise in manufacturing he had gained through his refrigerator company, he told the owner that he would like to become their exclusive manufacturer of motorcycle tire rims. The factory boss was taken back by Li's brazenness, and laughed that a state-owned factory of their size could never rely on such a small firm with no proven track record in the motorcycle industry. Similar to his earlier experience producing refrigerators, Li returned home determined not only to build motorcycle parts, but to build complete motorcycles. However, with no industry experience, his friends and family had little faith in his ability to succeed. It wasn't until Li bought a small state-owned motorcycle company that he finally acquired the necessary technology to produce his motorcycles – and he did so quite successfully. What began as a career running a photography studio switched to managing a burgeoning refrigerator company, and then transformed into creating a motorcycle company – but Li's most lucrative investment decision had yet to occur.

In the 1980s and 1990s, international automakers such as Volkswagen, General Motors, Honda and Nissan entered the Chinese auto market through government-brokered joint ventures and alliances in exchange for limited access to the companies' valuable intellectual property. By the early 2000s, their investment began to pay off and China's automotive market was booming. By 2009, China surpassed the US as the world's largest auto market. Previously, Chinese consumers considered buying a house their one major lifetime purchase, but car ownership was quickly becoming a newly desired "second essential." Li Shufu saw a great opportunity in China's auto industry, as most cars produced by international automakers were too expensive for typical Chinese consumers. He wanted to build cars that were more affordable for the average middle-class Chinese consumer. Always eager to take on a new challenge, Li famously said that a car is simply "four wheels and three sofas – how hard could it be to produce?" With that mindset, Li created Geely – which means "lucky" in Mandarin – and quickly built it into a successful Chinese car company based in Hangzhou, the capital of Zhejiang province. Li would not settle for Geely being an average Chinese car company. He wanted to acquire the world-class technology and achieve the brand recognition of an established global player, and he knew the way to do that was to acquire a premium automotive brand.[1]

Ever the ambitious visionary, Li had his sights set on Volvo early. Through Li's research, he had learned that Volvo was never a strategic brand for its American owner, Ford Motors. This is because Ford has been and remains primarily a mass-market car company; as a premium brand, Volvo was out of reach for many of Ford's target consumers.[2] As early as 2002, Li began contacting Ford, to try to convince them to take his intention to buy Volvo seriously. He sent letters to Ford's senior management and networked with them at auto shows, but without success. Li took his first trip to Ford's headquarters in Detroit to visit its Chief Financial Officer in 2007, but he did not receive a warm welcome. Instead, Li was met with concerns about his ability to raise sufficient capital for a deal, and was reminded of the fact that Geely was a relative unknown in the West. At the time of his first visit Volvo was not nearly as troubled as it was about to become, but Li had his heart set on acquiring the Volvo brand from Ford at all costs.

It wasn't until the 2008 global financial crisis occurred that Ford's leadership finally became receptive to Li's proposition. Li began to rack up miles on overseas flights to Detroit and Gothenburg, Sweden, where Volvo was based. To appease Volvo's senior management, Li committed early on to ensure Volvo's headquarters stayed in Sweden and its leadership team remained intact. Geely's acquisition of Volvo would keep 16,000 local employees at their jobs. Back in China,[3] Li communicated with regulatory authorities to make them aware of the potential acquisition and procedural obstacles before they arose later on to impede the deal's progress. Li effectively painted the picture of a win-win situation for all parties involved in the acquisition. In fact, many of Li's fellow Chinese automotive executives believe that one of the greatest talents he brings to the table is public relations.

Li also wooed the Swedish leadership team of Volvo by emphasizing the vast untapped potential of the Chinese auto market. He argued that while the US, Germany, and France had all been major markets for Volvo in the past, they were highly competitive and increasingly saturated. China was not only the world's largest auto market; it also had tremendous growth potential given China's historical absence of car ownership. There were 62 million automobiles on China's roads in 2009, a figure which some projected would grow to reach 200 million by 2020.[4] By selling China as the world's largest automobile market, Li helped create a path of opportunity for future growth, and a chance to make Volvo profitable in China. Li also underscored the potential for selling Volvo's European premium brand to China's growing population of luxury consumers. With Li offering the localized know-how to navigate the intricacies of doing business in China, Volvo's management saw how they could benefit from the acquisition by Geely.

In August 2010, the farm boy from Hangzhou, China, officially acquired the movie star from Gothenburg, Sweden, for $1.5 billion. By 2013, China became Volvo's most profitable market, where it produced 42,000 automobiles. Doug Speck, Senior Vice-President of Sales and Marketing for Volvo told the *Financial Times* in a 2013 interview: "We expect a significant bump-up from localization." Management expects annual sales to increase to 200,000 by 2015 after the Chinese government officially recognizes Volvo as a local firm through Geely's ownership in 2014.[5] Li Shufu fulfilled his commitment to open new markets for Volvo, while acquiring a global luxury car brand to help boost Geely's international image.

Chinese companies' international mergers and acquisitions

Li Shufu is only one among several Chinese businesspeople to emerge on the global stage as the result of a high-profile cross-border M&A deal. His ambition, drive and entrepreneurship embody the spirit of his fellow Chinese business leaders who built similarly successful companies, like Yang Yuanqing of Lenovo and Wang Zongnan of Bright Food. However, according to Peter Williamson, University of Cambridge professor and author of *Dragons at Your Door*, Chinese overseas M&A is still "a relatively new phenomenon in the global marketplace."[6] During the 1980s and for most of the 1990s, there was little to no outbound M&A activity. By the early 2000s, the first wave of Chinese overseas M&A involved acquiring overseas firms that were distressed and had big brands.

Such was the case for TCL, a Chinese technology company that merged its television and DVD business with France's Thomson in 2003. TCL forced the integration with Thomson to move too fast before winning over the French team, resulting in what industry experts called a "tremendous disaster." Shanghai Automotive Industry Corporation (SAIC) purchased Ssangyong Motors in 2004, after the Korean automotive firm became debilitated by the Asian financial crisis. But by buying up distressed foreign companies, Chinese firms set themselves up for failure from the beginning: how could Chinese companies with such limited overseas experience be able to breathe life into dying businesses that even domestic management could not revive? According to research by the US-based Brookings Institution, nearly 90 percent of the approximately 300 overseas M&A transactions made by Chinese firms between 2008 and 2010 failed, losing at least 40 percent of their initial purchase value.[7]

But, as Geely's acquisition of Volvo illustrates, the Chinese outbound M&A landscape is continuing to evolve and successful major deals are becoming more common. Two years after the Geely–Volvo acquisition, Chinese firms engaged in a number of high-profile deals in the US and EU. In 2012, Sany Heavy Industry, a Chinese producer of industrial machinery, offered to buy a 90 percent stake in German industrial firm Putzmeister for €360 million (approximately $475 million).[8] Through the acquisition, Sany transformed seemingly overnight into a global competitor with market leaders like US-based Caterpillar and Japan's Komatsu. In May of the same year, Shanghai's Bright Food, a diversified consumer goods company, acquired a controlling stake in Weetabix, a British breakfast cereal brand, in a £1.2 billion (approximately $1.9 billion) deal.[9] Then just a few weeks later, Dalian Wanda Group agreed to buy AMC Entertainment for $2.6 billion, marking the largest-ever buyout of a US company by a Chinese firm at that time.[10]

To answer the question posed by the title of this chapter, Chinese firms are not "buying up the world's corporations." However, they are assuming an increasingly prominent role in the global M&A space. The following sections examine the unique challenges Chinese companies encounter when pursuing M&A; explain how M&A acts as a primary method to realize commercially driven motivations for international expansion; and provide examples of Chinese firms that have successfully acquired and integrated Western firms.

M&A: the preferred path to Chinese firms' foreign investment in the West

When Chinese companies expand overseas, they have three primary options. The first option is what industry experts refer to as a "greenfield investment," an investment made by a company to establish and directly manage a new overseas operation. An example of a greenfield investment would be if ChemChina were to build a new chemical factory in South Carolina in the US or in Coburg, Germany. The second option is a partnership or joint venture with an established Western multinational. This form of investment allows the Chinese firm to gain exposure to the Western market through its partner's existing brand name and capabilities. At first, Goldwind established a partnership with Germany's Vensys. After partnering on a range of initiatives for three years, the Chinese wind energy firm selected the third option, merger and acquisition (M&A), acquiring a 70 percent stake in Vensys. M&A is when a Chinese firm buys partial or full ownership of a Western firm. After the acquisition, the Western firm becomes part of the Chinese company. Although, as the examples in the following sections illustrate, the extent to which the Western firm integrates into the Chinese company will vary depending on the acquirer's post-acquisition strategy. Chinese firms increasingly choose M&A as the preferred form of foreign direct investment in the US and EU (Figure 5.1).

The data for both the US and EU reveals a steady increase in both the quantity of M&A deals taking place as well as the size of the investments. M&A is often the most attractive strategy for Chinese firms because it offers them new market access, increased capabilities in the form of managerial and technical know-how, and global brand recognition.

Challenges Chinese firms face in overseas M&A

According to Richard Leggett, Chief Executive Officer of Frontier Strategy Group and former Managing Director at Goldman Sachs, less than half of M&A attempts are successful – and the success rate for overseas acquisitions is even worse. Leggett explains: "Multinational executives acquiring companies in overseas markets confront a wide range of challenges, especially in the post-merger integration phase when two very different national and corporate

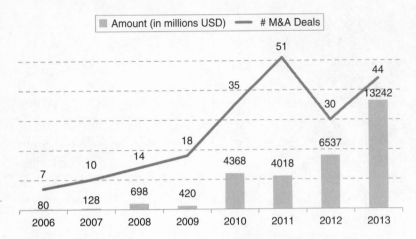

FIGURE 5.1   Chinese M&A in the United States (2006–2013)
Source: Author's image, China Investment Tracker, Rhodium Group data.

cultures must come together." He suggests that companies should assess possible risks ahead of time and create plans for different potential scenarios that could unfold after the deal goes through. "Given the low success rate of cross border M&A attempts this is the best strategy a company can employ to minimize the substantial risk associated with their investment." Like their Western counterparts, Chinese firms face obstacles across each stage of the M&A process – from initial assessment of potential acquisition targets, to the auction and bidding process, to post-merger integration of the Western firm into its China-based corporate organization. While Chinese companies face all of the same challenges that any company taking part in an overseas M&A deal may encounter, there are several factors that make their situation unique.[11]

> M&A is often the most attractive strategy for Chinese firms because it offers them new market access, increased capabilities in the forms of managerial and technical know-how, and global brand recognition.

Managing the auction process

Michael Pettis, a professor at Peking University's Guanghua School of Management, recounts one of the first finance courses he ever took while studying with a prominent professor from Princeton in the early 1980s. "At the time there were many mergers and acquisitions taking place and spectacular articles in the newspaper about how brilliant it was that Company X bought Company Y. My professor pointed out that it is really easy to win an acquisition – that step only involves being willing to pay more than anyone else."[12] Applying this insight to Chinese companies taking part in the auction process to buy a Western company is highly relevant, because it suggests Chinese firms are willing to pay significantly higher prices to win deals. In 2013, investment bank J.P. Morgan found that Chinese acquirers paid a 33 percent premium when acquiring assets located in North America, compared to a 25 percent premium paid by acquirers from other nations.[13] Regardless of the location, M&A advisory experts interviewed for this book who facilitate Chinese overseas deals in the West unanimously agree that Chinese companies pay significantly more when acquiring companies in advanced economies. Why is this the case?

The high bidding price required of Chinese companies by Western firms is primarily due to the increased uncertainty of whether a deal will go through when a Chinese buyer is involved. Many Chinese executives lack experience bidding on major overseas M&A deals – for some it may even be their first time. According to China business veteran Jack Perkowski, Managing Director of JFP Holdings and author of *Managing the Dragon*, Chinese executives have a very difficult time understanding and navigating the overseas M&A auction process. He explains how a Chinese executive may receive a "teaser" from an investment bank about an acquisition target and a non-disclosure agreement (NDA) that he or she must sign in order to receive an Information Memorandum. In the same package, the Chinese executive may also be notified that an initial indication of interest is due in two weeks time if he or she wishes to proceed to the next step.

While the initial bidding process detailed above would likely be just as challenging for an inexperienced buyer from a country like Malaysia or South Korea, the high bidding price required for Chinese acquirers is also related to factors unique to China. Perkowski explains: "Obtaining the necessary approvals to go forward with a deal, or to convert *renminbi* into foreign currency, can be time consuming and problematic." The necessary time required to interact with the multiple government agencies introduced in Chapter 1 can delay a Chinese firm's ability to submit a bid on time. Additionally, because the Chinese *renminbi* is not readily convertible into foreign exchange, Chinese buyers may face additional delays coordinating with authorities from the State Administration of Foreign Exchange (SAFE). The complexity and unpredictable nature of the Chinese government approval process, combined with Chinese buyers' general lack of experience in cross-border M&A, have led Western investment bankers to require higher bidding prices to compensate for the additional risk associated with selecting a Chinese buyer.[14]

Management visits

If the Chinese firm does progress successfully through the auction process, the next stage is likely to be a management visit in which its senior executives travel to the headquarters of the company being acquired to meet with their top management. Visas are mundane but often very real initial obstacles in this process, because Chinese executives cannot travel to the US and the EU without them. The necessary time required to process a visa through the appropriate embassies and consulates, in addition to lengthy flight times from China, may make it very cumbersome for the Chinese company's leaders to travel to the overseas office. Perkowski notes: "While it's easy for a CEO in Chicago to schedule a trip to meet the management of a company in St. Louis, it's a much longer trip for a Chinese CEO, and the need for a visa makes last-minute trips all but impossible."

Once the Chinese executive team finally arrives in a location like Peach Tree City, Georgia, or Kettering, UK, where their acquisition target is based, both executive teams may face cultural and communication difficulties throughout the course of their time together. Yet critical decisions must be made based on the information communicated within this short period. "The idea of buying a company only four months after you first meet the management is a completely counter-Chinese way of doing business," says Perkowski. In general, Chinese management prefers to build relationships and trust with potential business partners that can take years to develop. Moreover, the integration process following the acquisition may lead to further challenges – from negotiations with labor unions, to poor initial business performance, to unanticipated regulatory hurdles.[15]

Post-merger integration

After acquiring a Western firm, a Chinese company can either choose to invest capital in the Western business but adopt a relatively "hands-off" approach to managing the existing organization, or the Chinese firm can integrate the Western company into its own organization. Because the primary interests of Chinese firms acquiring Western firms are often new markets, expanded capabilities and international brands, many companies prefer the first option. In this situation, the Chinese company allows the Western firm to operate relatively independently, like it did prior to the acquisition, with limited interference from the Chinese side. This was the approach adopted with German manufacturer Waldrich Coburg and American automotive component manufacturer Nexteer, both introduced in Chapter 7, as well as with many of the examples later in this chapter.

Alternatively, a Chinese company may seek to integrate management teams and core business functions such as finance and human resources, merging both sides into a single organization. But in this scenario, the management teams may realize they are "in the same bed, but have different dreams." This phrase refers to the Chinese idiom *tongchuang yimeng* (同床异梦), which long-time China watcher James McGregor uses to describe the relationship between Chinese and Western business partners in his book, *One Billion Customers*.[16] When applied to business, the idiom can be used to describe the situation of two business partners engaged in a single venture, but who possess two divergent visions for their company's future development. The Chinese firm may come to realize that it will take significantly more management time and investment to make the joint business work, ultimately leading to a failed acquisition.

Chinese business expansion through M&A

Chapter 2 introduced the political and business motivations for Chinese companies' global expansion. M&A is a natural means for Chinese businesses to achieve their goals of new market access, increased capabilities in the forms of managerial and technical know-how, and global brand recognition. The examples in the following sections illustrate how despite the challenges Chinese companies face in their attempts at overseas M&A, more and more companies are learning from their own and others' mistakes to successfully fulfill their commercial ambitions for new markets, capabilities, and brands.

Buying new markets

"Sany was love at first sight," remarked Norbert Scheuch, Chief Executive Officer of Putzmeister.[17] Putzmeister is a German industrial company that produces specialized cement-pump machines that have been used for major projects like Dubai's Khalifa Tower and reviving Japan's Fukushima region after the devastating 2011 earthquake. Despite its status as Germany's largest cement-pump maker, the firm was hit hard by the global financial crisis, witnessing its annual revenues cut in half in 2009 and forced to lay off hundreds of workers. For Scheuch and Putzmeister, it was time to think about how to save the troubled industrial giant, and the best way seemed to be through seeking out potential investors. Liang Wengen, Chairman of Sany Heavy Industry, China's largest construction equipment group, came to their rescue. In January 2011, Sany Heavy made its first overseas acquisition by purchasing a 90 percent stake in Putzmeister for an estimated €360 million (approximately $475 million).

For Sany, the acquisition was extremely effective in advancing its efforts to increase market share outside of China and internationalize its business. Prior to the deal, Sany's overseas sales made up just four percent of its revenue. In contrast, more than 80 percent of Putzmeister's revenue came from overseas – from countries other than China. Technology gained through the acquisition also gave Sany a competitive boost in developed markets, explains Tony Nash, Vice President at consulting firm IHS. He notes: "There is no doubt that key Putzmeister technology is being folded into Sany Heavy's product lines, with German R&D complemented by Chinese manufacturing scale." Through the investment in Putzmeister, Sany increased its overseas sales four-fold, acquired a global distribution and service network, and positioned itself to become a serious competitor to incumbent industry leaders, US-based Caterpillar and Japan's Komatsu.

But Sany's success in winning over the various stakeholders involved in the acquisition was not simply a matter of money. To appease Putzmeister's 3,000 employees, and avoid roadblocks from local unions in Germany, Sany promised job security and agreed to postpone layoffs resulting from the acquisition until 2020. To appeal to the German firm's nationalistic spirit, Sany also agreed to use the Putzmeister brand in all of its international markets outside of China. Nash notes: "Sany will move its headquarters for concrete equipment to Germany, further boosting its legitimacy and at the same time gaining a meaningful foothold in one of the world's largest and most respected markets." Finally, Scheuch would remain CEO of Putzmeister, guiding the company through the transition and helping to achieve Sany's goal of an estimated $2.7 billion (€2 billion) in revenues by 2016, up from approximately $920 million (€700 million) in 2012. He would also be named to Sany's Board of Directors, which had previously been comprised of predominantly Chinese executives, in order to further internationalize Sany's business.[18]

Buying new capabilities for the domestic market

Not all overseas acquisitions by Chinese companies focus on gaining market share in international markets. Chinese firms also buy established global players to become more competitive in the massive domestic Chinese market, where they now face intense competition from fellow Chinese companies in addition to Western multinational firms operating in China. Gaining access to cutting edge technology and international managerial know-how can provide the acquiring Chinese firm with a competitive advantage over both local and foreign rivals in China. In some cases, the overseas acquisition may be in an area completely different from the core business of the Chinese firm; however, it may be an area of strategic potential in the domestic market.

The market opportunity for luxury goods in China is tremendous. China is currently the world's second largest luxury goods market, and McKinsey & Company estimates that China will account for $27 billion or 20 percent of global luxury sales by 2015.[19] However, luxury consumption is not solely limited to Louis Vuitton purses and Omega watches. The China Boat Industry and Trade Association (CBITA) estimates that the Chinese recreational boat market will be worth as much as $10 billion over the next decade.[20] In China, these expensive vessels are used primarily to entertain guests, clients and family members rather than to travel luxuriously around the world. International yacht manufacturers have begun entering the Chinese market as demand increases in large coastal regions, including the Pearl River Delta and Yangtze River Delta in the south and Bohai Bay in northeast China.

Ferretti Group, the world's largest yacht builder, recognized the vast market potential in China early on. It opened its first representative office in Shanghai in 2005 to build and manage its customer and sales networks. Building on its 43 years of experience in the luxury yacht space, the China market was already contributing approximately 10 percent of Ferretti's annual revenues. However, Ferretti faced ongoing financial challenges outside China, especially back home in Europe. It had been battling bankruptcy since 2007 and was struggling to stay afloat in the wake of the eurozone crisis. Ferretti's debt-laden operations could only be rescued by a buyer willing to come to bail out the company financially. It just so happened that this buyer was not a yacht maker, nor was it a producer of any sort of marine vehicle – Ferretti's savior came in the form of a Chinese state-owned bulldozer maker.

Shandong Heavy, a Chinese industrial giant with international ambitions, invested approximately €374 million (around $478 million) for a 75 percent stake in Ferretti in January 2012. Shandong Heavy acquired a controlling share in the Italian yacht maker to obtain valuable technology and managerial know-how to capitalize on China's luxury market. Tan Xuguang, Chairman of Shandong Heavy, was quoted in the official press release as saying: "Developing the yacht business is one of [Shandong Heavy's] strategic goals for the next five years. Ferretti, which possesses iconic international brands, state-of-the-art manufacturing technologies, products of the highest quality and an extensive sales network, is an ideal partner." The major driver of Shandong Heavy's investment in Ferretti was clearly an interest in buying international capabilities in an emerging strategic area of the Chinese luxury market – capabilities in the form of valuable technology to build world-class yachts as well as the expertise to build and manage a luxury lifestyle brand in China.[21]

> Chinese firms also buy established global players to become more competitive in the massive domestic Chinese market, where they now face intense competition.

Buying global brands

Headlines about big name Chinese acquisitions in the West like the Lenovo–IBM deal are no longer a rare occurrence. Headlines such as "Cereal owner Weetabix to get Chinese Owner," "Wanda Group of China buys AMC Entertainment," and "China's Geely buys Volvo for $1.5bn" are now published more often than ever before. The increasing frequency of big brand acquisitions is no accident. In 2012, Chinese Premier Wen Jiabao highlighted strategic industries in China whose globalization efforts the government intends to promote. These industries include: next generation information technology, energy and mining, automobiles, home appliances, financial services, equipment manufacturing, construction, internet technology, and medicine. With regard to the consumer goods sector, Premier Wen instructed Chinese brands to "seek to expand market experience and build talent reserves acquiring international luxury brands in order to enter the global consumer market."[22] Given the number of years and resources required to build a global brand through one's own efforts, M&A is a key means to help propel a Chinese company's brand into the lives of international consumers.

Perhaps one of the most intriguing brand acquisitions made to date by a Chinese firm is the acquisition of 80-year-old UK breakfast cereal brand Weetabix by China's state-owned food conglomerate Bright Food. Weetabix, a long-time family owned company, was bought out by a Texas private equity firm and eventually sold to Lion Capital in 2004. Given its strong cash position, Bright Food acquired a controlling stake in Weetabix from Lion Capital in May 2012. At the time of the acquisition, Weetabix exported to over 80 countries, and had approximately 2,000 employees with annual sales in excess of about £1.2 billion (approximately $1.9 billion).[23]

While UK consumers have shown a long-time love for the crispy wheat cereal, it seems unlikely that Chinese consumers will develop a taste for Weetabix anytime soon. Typical Chinese breakfast options include favorites like *youtiao*, crispy fried dough sticks dipped in soymilk, or a hot rice congee called *zhou*. Chinese consumers have yet to embrace mainstream global cereal brands from companies like General Mills or the Kellogg Company, and it is unlikely that Weetabix will be any more successful in appealing to the taste buds of Chinese consumers. All signs suggest that the Weetabix acquisition was aimed first and foremost at acquiring the long-established Weetabix brand name to sell internationally, rather than marketing the cereal in China's domestic market.

In fact, Wang Zongnan, Chairman of Shanghai-based Bright Food, has clearly expressed the company's aspirations to internationalize its business operations and expand its global supply chain of food products. Wang intends to increase overseas sales contribution to overall revenue from 5 percent in 2012, to 30 percent by 2017.[24] To achieve this ambitious goal, Bright Food plans to acquire long-term established brands across strategic areas such as dairy, sugar and alcohol. Such acquisitions will also provide Bright Food with on-the-ground marketing capabilities to further extend its influence in international markets. The Weetabix acquisition was its most successful to-date, as Bright Food had faced serious setbacks in its earlier overseas acquisition attempts in the UK and Europe. In September 2010, it failed to acquire United Biscuits, maker of UK consumer favorites like Jaffa Cakes and Hula Hoops. In January 2011, Bright Food put in an unsuccessful bid for US-based GNC Nutrition in its attempt to enter the retail nutrition business. Later that March, Bright Food lost a bidding war over Yoplait to General Mills, despite reportedly offering more money than the US-based food group. It wasn't until August 2011 that Bright Food finally made progress in its overseas M&A expansion plans, successfully acquiring a 75 percent stake in Australia's Manassen Foods for $516 million.[25]

Bright Food's global brand acquisition strategy is a smart move, especially since it is itself a consumer-facing brand. It can take decades to build a globally recognizable brand; in the case of Weetabix, nearly a century. It would take years for Chinese companies to carefully build their brands in international markets. While this is certainly their long-term strategy, in the short-term, acquisitions of established brands give Chinese firms immediate gains by obtaining the brand equity needed to successfully expand and operate overseas. By "piggy-backing" on the reputations of established international brands, Chinese companies can further penetrate global markets and acquire new customers.

Key takeaways from this chapter

While the phenomenon of Chinese companies buying firms in the West is relatively new, it will continue to grow in importance in the years to come. In a post-global financial crisis environment in which many developed economies remain relatively weak and long-established firms have faltered, Chinese overseas M&A's will only continue to increase in size and frequency. A series of record-breaking acquisitions occurred in 2012 alone. In May, Dalian Wanda's acquisition of AMC theaters marked the largest Chinese acquisition of an American firm at $2.6 billion. In December, China National Offshore Oil Company (CNOOC) broke global M&A records with its $15.1 billion acquisition of Canada's Nexen in the oil and gas sector.[26] As these and the examples of Geely, Sany, and Bright Food illustrate, the advantages of acquisitions over greenfield investments are clear. Through overseas M&A, Chinese firms gain immediate access to new markets, capabilities, and brands. At the same time, Chinese firms will need to embrace new ways of doing business, such as the M&A auction process and the integration of vastly different corporate cultures into a single entity with a shared set of values and business practices.

Part *III*

The Issues

The Concerns: Should the West Worry about Chinese Investment?

Charles Ding and Zhu Jingyun stare at each other across the room as they await the start of Congressional hearings on September 13, 2012. It's a cool autumn morning on Capitol Hill, Washington DC, and the two business executives wonder why the United States House Intelligence Committee selected their firms as targets of an extensive investigation. Ding is a Senior Vice President and the chief US representative for Huawei, a telecommunications company with operations around the world worth an estimated $35 billion in 2013.[1] Two years earlier, Ding had moved his family to Bethesda, Maryland, after nearly 17 years with the firm in China. Zhu leads the North American and European operations for ZTE, a $13 billion[2] Chinese competitor of Huawei. The United States House Intelligence Committee had seemingly grouped Huawei and ZTE together as part of the investigation because both companies operate in the telecommunications industry, originate from China, and are expanding rapidly in overseas markets in the developed and developing world.

Huawei has been fighting for years to shed its image of a company controlled by the Chinese state, despite its private ownership structure. Huawei founder and CEO Ren Zhengfei's past experience in China's People's Liberation Army (PLA) is often cited by overseas media and officials to suggest that Huawei collaborates with the Chinese government. As a result, Huawei has worked tirelessly over the last decade to shed this impression, partnering with global public relations firms, advertisers, and strategic counsel. Huawei more than quadrupled its expenditure on lobbying activities in Washington building up to the proceedings. The firm spent a total of $820,000 on government lobbying in the first 6 months of 2012 alone.[3] Huawei even went so far as to hire former UK government chief information officer, John Suffolk, to serve as its first global cyber security officer in 2011. In an official press release from Huawei, Ren explains: "We have never sold any key equipment to major US carriers, nor have we sold any equipment to any US government agency. Huawei has no connection to the cyber security issues the US has encountered in the past, current and future."[4]

Zhu's ZTE is a publicly traded company, listed both on China's Shenzhen stock exchange and on the Hong Kong stock exchange. Its products include consumer electronics, videoconferencing devices, and high-speed internet networking equipment. ZTE is a third the size of Huawei, but because it also operates in the telecommunications industry it shares many of the political and regulatory hurdles encountered by its larger Chinese competitor. Journalists often cite the two firms together in articles about potential cyber security concerns posed by Chinese technology companies operating overseas. Reports also link both companies to telecommunications equipment sales to governments unfriendly to the US, like Iran. At the same time, lingering concerns remain about the degree of political influence the Chinese government has over Huawei and ZTE's businesses. It was therefore no surprise to some observers that the United States House Intelligence Committee chose to include both firms in its investigation.

As the day's session begins, Ding stands to deliver his opening remarks, peering above his rimless glasses and looking confidently into the eyes of each member of the congressional committee. His English is fluent, which is not a given for a veteran Chinese senior executive of his generation. His detailed remarks, available online, look to have been prepared by a professional public relations firm. His included biography looks like that of any senior executive at a leading multinational company, including a professional photo and detailed career history. Ding's team has clearly done their homework in advance of the hearing, preparing an opening statement addressing key issues including ownership structure, cyber security and the firm's investments in the US. Ding vehemently concludes: "Huawei has not and will not jeopardize our global commercial success nor the integrity of our customers' networks for any third party, government or otherwise. Ever."[5]

When ZTE's Zhu takes the stage, there is a clear shift in tone. The 38-year-old executive is visibly uncomfortable addressing such a high-level Western audience in English. He grips his papers with both hands and carefully reads each word. Rather than speaking directly about ZTE and its operations, he goes off on a tangent about the company's origins in the special economic zone of Shenzhen and "the spirit of Shenzhen." Both his written remarks and biography submitted to the Committee look to have been prepared by a Chinese translation firm: the grammar and sentence structure are poor, and there are many uses of colloquial language. Zhu argues that ZTE should not be under regulatory scrutiny because his firm's investments in the US are relatively insignificant. He reads aloud: "Sales of ZTE's telecom infrastructure equipment in the United States comprised less than $30 million in revenue last year. Two Western vendors, alone, last year provided the US market with $14 billion dollars' worth of equipment. ZTE should not be a focus of investigation to the exclusion of much larger Western vendors."[6]

After hours of answering questions from Committee members through translators, Congressman Mike Rogers gives closing remarks. "It is our job and responsibility to ensure that the networks of the United States meet our national security standards for the protection of the American people. I can say I'm a little disappointed today, I was hoping for more transparency, more directness ... there is a center and sphere of government influence in your companies of which you either can't identify their roles and responsibilities or won't. Either way is unacceptable when you're talking about entrusting millions of sensitive bits of information from US citizens and our companies."[7] It was therefore little surprise that one month later the Committee's formal report concluded that Huawei and ZTE both pose potential national security risks. According to the official report: "In sum the Committee finds that the companies failed to provide evidence that would satisfy any fair and full investigation. Although this alone does not prove wrongdoing, it factors into the Committee's conclusions ... The investigation concludes that the risks associated with Huawei's and ZTE's provision of equipment to US critical infrastructure could undermine core US national-security interests."[8]

What should the West be concerned about?

In theory, Chinese investment – like investment from any other country – should be welcomed in the West. The opportunity it offers to save struggling domestic firms, add jobs and tax dollars to local economies, and open up new markets overseas are all potential benefits associated with foreign direct investment from investors of any nationality. However, there are also legitimate concerns that one must be aware of before opening the door too wide to foreign investors. Huawei and ZTE have been, fairly or unfairly, grouped together as representing the national interests of the Chinese government in an extension of its influence in foreign markets including the US, EU, and Australia. Given the relatively short history of Chinese firms operating in the global marketplace, many of these concerns are not yet grounded in concrete evidence as much as they are based on speculation and fear about what could happen down the line. Eric C. Anderson, a faculty member with the US National Intelligence University and author of *Sinophobia: The Huawei Story*, argues that most people believe "it's not about what Chinese firms are doing today, it's about what they could do in the future." After Anderson's extensive research into Huawei, he believes the firm does not pose a threat to national security, but he also acknowledges that no one can predict what the firm could potentially do in the future under different circumstances.[9] In addition to national security, there is a wide range of economic and social concerns that should also be considered as part of the Chinese investment debate.

> There are also legitimate concerns that one must be aware of before opening the door too wide to foreign investors.

Deng Xiaoping, China's great economic reformer, encouraged market liberalization and investment from the West, but he was far from naïve about its consequences. He famously remarked, *dakai chuanghu, xinxian kongqi hui jinlai, cangying ye hui fei jinlai* (打开窗户，新鲜空气会进来，苍蝇也会飞进来) – "when you open a window, fresh air will come in, but so will some flies."[10] Deng recognized that foreign investment in China was necessary to build its economy; however, he also understood that foreign investment would bring negative consequences along with economic benefits. The West should learn from Deng's realistic approach. Chapter 7 introduces the political, economic and social benefits to foreign investment, but it is unrealistic to suggest that Chinese investment (or any nation's outbound investment) will bring only positive outcomes without the potential for disruptions to local political, economic, and social spheres.

Overcoming the "liability of foreignness"

In modern day Europe, a company like Coca-Cola may not seem as much "American" as it is "global." Similarly, a company like Siemens in the US does not necessarily trigger thoughts of "Made in Germany." Yet this wasn't always the case for these firms. In the 1960s, Coca-Cola faced difficulties in Europe when its overseas expansion was perceived as a form of corporate colonization or American cultural imperialism. The term *coca-colonization* was even coined out of fears that the company spread American cultural values through its overseas business operations and was in conflict with local cultures. The anti-American camp went so far as to insist that Coca-Cola's extensive distribution network allowed it to help the American government spy overseas.[11] As recently as 2005, then German Vice-Chancellor Franz Müntefering famously and controversially described foreign investors as "locusts."[12]

Like Coca-Cola, Chinese companies need to overcome what international business experts refer to as the "liability of foreignness," interpreted as the domestic concerns associated with a foreign company's presence in an overseas market. Such concerns can come in many forms, ranging from national security to unfair business practices to potential environmental costs. As a result, Chinese and other foreign companies are often put at a disadvantage before they even begin to operate overseas. Language and cultural differences only add to the perceived "foreignness" of investors, making it more difficult to overcome the negative perceptions of overseas stakeholders. A foreign firm may not be viewed as "less foreign," and its presence accepted as a net benefit to the local economy, until it demonstrates long-term responsible investment in the overseas country.[13] At least in the short term, Chinese companies face a wide range of Western worries across political, economic, and social realms.

The following sections in this chapter consider each of the following concerns related to Chinese investment in the West (Table 6.1).

It is important to be aware of the potential negative aspects of Chinese investment in order for a country to leverage its policy-making apparatus to create an effective screen letting positive investment through, while blocking the occasional negative 'flies'. Only by implementing a clear and consistent approach will governments in the West be able to screen and

Table 6.1 Concerns related to Chinese investment in the West

Political	Economic	Social
National security	Unfair competition	Labor standards
Cyber-security	Intellectual property theft	Consumer protection
Natural resources	Job & company relocation	Environmental protection
China trust gap	Economic reciprocity	

identify which Chinese investors and types of investment are welcome, and which are not.

Political concerns

While Sany Chairman Liang Wengen was purchasing Germany's Putzmeister, his firm continued to seek additional potential overseas acquisitions in developed markets. Liang sent two of his top executives to the US to identify potential opportunities to expand his firm's wind energy capabilities. Duan Dawei, Sany's Chief Financial Officer, and Wu Jialing, General Manager of the firm's electrical division, traveled to the US and incorporated a Delaware-based holding company under the name "Ralls Corporation." By March 2012, one month before the Putzmeister acquisition was officially completed, Duan and Wu had acquired rights to build a wind farm in Oregon. But the Sany executives had neglected to first engage an experienced third party on the ground who would have advised Sany to first submit the proposed deal to the Committee on Foreign Investment in the United States (CFIUS) for review. CFIUS possesses the authority to review and investigate any foreign investment in the US with potential national security implications. The advisor would have informed Duan and Wu, that while they could proceed with the acquisition without informing CFIUS, it would not be wise do so, given the potential political sensitivity of foreign investment in industries like energy and telecommunications, or in certain locations in the US.

By not first submitting their proposed investment to CFIUS, Sany had left the door wide open for a federal investigation to enter – which is exactly what happened. What Duan and Wu didn't realize was that the rights they had acquired were for land in close proximity to a US naval base. CFIUS found what it concluded to be "credible evidence" that Sany's investment near a US military facility posed a threat to US national security. After Sany unsuccessfully challenged the CFIUS ruling, President Barack Obama issued an executive order blocking the deal from going through – the first presidential order blocking a foreign company's investment in the US in over 20 years.[14]

While Sany's proposed wind energy deal required exceptional presidential intervention, it was not the first Chinese investment in the US to be blocked by the CFIUS process on grounds of national security. The first high-profile case involving a Chinese company occurred in 2005, when China National Offshore Oil Corporation (CNOOC) attempted to take over American oil and gas firm Unocal.[15] Subsequently in 2008 and 2011, two attempted Huawei investments in American technology firms 3Com and 3Leaf Systems, were also challenged by CFIUS.[16] Followed in 2012 by the Sany–Ralls case and the Mandiant report filed against Huawei and ZTE, the US began to appear a less receptive place for Chinese investment in certain industries. Why is this the case?

National security is cited as the primary political concern related to Chinese and other foreign investment in the US, and it is indeed a vital consideration. Yet critics of CFIUS argue that its review processes lack transparency and predictability, and discriminate against companies of certain nationalities. Chapter 8 identifies several areas where the current process could be improved. Most legal advisory firms recommend that Chinese companies submit any investment in politically sensitive industries or areas to CFIUS in advance to ensure the deal is structured appropriately and to minimize chances that it will be blocked. CFIUS has 30 days to review a transaction before notifying the parties involved that their proposed investment "threatens to impair the national security of the United States." If CFIUS members do not reach a unanimous decision within the first 30 days, the investigation can be extended to 45 days.[17]

In addition to CFIUS, the US Department of Justice (DOJ) and Federal Trade Commission (FTC) also play important roles to ensure that Chinese investment does not infringe on the competitiveness of American firms. In particular the DOJ and FTC are involved to prevent anticompetitive mergers or acquisitions from taking place. In addition to these formal processes, individual American politicians may also influence which companies can buy American firms and operate in the US. For example, when Shuanghui International announced its intention to acquire Smithfield Foods, several congressional representatives took an open stance against the acquisition and proposed a new bill that would add further scrutiny to the deal beyond the standard CFIUS review. Connecticut congresswoman Rosa DeLauro called upon her fellow public officials to support additional review measures: "Smithfield's potential acquisition by a Chinese company raises important questions about intellectual property rights, food safety and public health, among other issues. Public officials have a responsibility to protect American consumers and businesses. That includes ensuring a fair economic playing field and the safety and security of our food supply." DeLauro had no prior experience dealing with international business, but claims of potential food safety and public health concerns were aligned with her role as the ranking member dealing with appropriations for Labor, Health, Human Services, and Education.[18]

Current regulatory bodies in the US, as well as in other developed markets, administer varying levels of review and oversight. In general, Western economies tend to have a three-part regulatory process for screening inbound foreign investment (FDI). First, competition policy authorities assess potential anti-competitive consequences of cross-border mergers and acquisitions. Second, there is a body like CFIUS that screens FDI for potential national security risks. Third, selected governments, especially in Europe, institute industry-specific regulations to prevent investment in industries deemed "national" or "strategic."[19] However, existing regulatory apparatuses could be improved to ensure greater operational clarity and consistency in case handling. Western nations, as with many host countries receiving inbound foreign direct investment, tend to intentionally structure their regulatory processes to allow for flexibility relating to when and where they allow FDI into their economies.[20] The following section introduces the different regulatory bodies across other key geographies in the West where Chinese companies are investing.

The European Union does not have a unified security screening body similar to CFIUS; however, most member states have their own national security review processes. France has the "Danone Law" (see next section), which went into effect in 2005 after fears that its national champions would be acquired by American and other European companies. And Germany's

Table 6.2 Laws and policies regulating foreign investment in the West

Country	Year enacted	Review process and key regulations
United States	1975	• Committee on Foreign Investment in the United States (CFIUS) • Department of Justice (DOJ), Federal Trade Commission (FTC) • Foreign Investment and National Security Act (FINSA) of 2007 • Exon-Florio Amendment of 1988 (Presidential authority to block deals on grounds of national security)
France	2005	• Ministry of Economy, Finance and Employment led review • Decree No. 2005-1739 aka "Danone Law," 2005 Decree 11 sectors
Germany	2009	• Federal Ministry of Economics and Technology (FMoET) • German Foreign Trade and Payments Act (Section 7)
Australia	1975	• Foreign Investment Review Board (FIRB) • Foreign Acquisitions and Takeovers Act (FATA)
Canada	1985	• Industry Canada, Ministry of Industry • Investment Canada Act (ICA)

Foreign Trade and Payments Act 2009 protects against potential national security threats. The Foreign Investment Review Board (FIRB) of Australia, and Canada's *Investment Canada Act*, co-managed by Industry Canada and the Ministry of Industry, aims to ensure foreign investment yields a "net benefit" to their respective nations. However, a key fact to note is that approximately 14 countries in the EU do not have national security review processes in place. These member states are predominantly in central and eastern Europe. Under the current EU regulatory structure, foreign firms that may not gain access to France or Germany may still have the ability to invest in countries like Hungary or Bulgaria, produce goods there, and then export them freely to other EU member states in the EU single market (Table 6.2).

National security: perception versus reality

In August 2013, Brett Lambert, then Deputy Assistant Secretary of Defense for US Manufacturing and Industrial Policy, told the media: "You have foreign capital that wants to come in, which we want, which we encourage. The question is how do we allow that foreign capital to come in while protecting national security." During the press conference, Lambert urged foreign businesses and governments to look at the data when assessing America's openness to outside investment and not to just look at headlines.[21] Lambert is right to say so, as the number of deals that actually experience setbacks in the US are minimal compared to the ones that are successful, and Chinese investments constitute a minority of these cases. The most recent CFIUS report to Congress found that of the 111 transactions submitted to CFIUS in 2011, 40 transactions (approximately 36 percent) required an investigation and only six investors withdrew their intent to invest once it was apparent that CFIUS might block their deal. The vast majority of the cases submitted to CFIUS from 2009 to 2011 were not even from emerging economies like China (20), but from advanced economies like the UK (68), France (27) and Canada (27).[22]

The same holds true in Australia, a developed market that employs a national security screening approach similar to the US. According to research conducted by Arthur Kroeber of GaveKal Dragonomics: "In 2009, the Australian Foreign Investment Review Board reviewed 106 cases of overseas Chinese direct investment. Of these, 101 passed through, 5 had question marks and 1 was told quietly that it would not be a good idea to proceed. In short, more than 90 percent were going through with little difficulty."[23] The most notable failure of Chinese investment in Australia was a proposed $19.5 billion stake in Australian mining firm Rio Tinto by Chinese state-owned resources group Chinalco. Otherwise, cases of challenged Chinese investments in Australia are even fewer than those in the US (Table 6.3).

Table 6.3 Highly quoted challenged Chinese investments in the West

Company	Year	Country	Detail
CNOOC	2005	United States	$18.5 billion for Unocal, oil and gas
Haier	2005	United States	$1.3 billion for Maytag, washing machines
Chinalco	2009	Australia	$19.5 billion stake in Rio Tinto Group, mining firm
Huawei	2008	United States	$2.2 billion for 3Com, internet router and networking equipment firm
Huawei	2011	United States	$2 million for 3Leaf Systems, server firm
Sany-Ralls	2012	United States	$20 million for Oregon wind farm project
Shuanghui	2013	United States	$4.7 billion for Smithfield Foods, pork production

Negative perceptions of the potential 'threat' posed by Chinese investment are amplified by media coverage focused on a very small number of failed cases. As a result this generates a perception among Chinese executives that "Chinese investment is not welcome in the US." Few news stories look back at a company like CNOOC that initially faced challenges expanding overseas in 2005 and examines how it has improved with experience. By taking minority stakes in key investments and ensuring it follows the required review processes, CNOOC went on to invest over $2 billion in both US-based Chesapeake Energy in 2010[24] and Canada's Opti in 2011.[25] It then invested $15.1 billion to acquire Canada's Nexen, a deal Canadian Prime Minister Stephen Harper cited as a net benefit to Canada's economy compared to a jettisoned 2010 investment involving Australian mining giant BHP Billiton.[26] Overly politicizing the handful of failed deals generates negative perceptions among Chinese firms as well as domestic publics about Chinese investment in the West. Ultimately this may lead to a situation in which a Chinese firm that would otherwise invest in the US or Australia instead chooses Nigeria or Saudi Arabia which have better reputations for welcoming Chinese investment.

> Negative perceptions of the potential 'threat' posed by Chinese investment are amplified by media coverage focused on a very small number of failed cases.

Economic concerns

Between Bright Food's purchase of a majority stake in New Zealand's Synlait and its successful acquisition of the UK's Weetabix, the firm set its sights on France's number two yogurt brand, Yoplait. Interestingly, the yogurt industry has proven to be one of the most contentious areas of foreign direct investment in the French economy. A 2005 rumor that US-based PepsiCo intended to acquire Danone, the number one yogurt producer in France, raised concerns among French political elite that its "national champion" might be taken over by an American company.

French Prime Minister Dominique de Villepin remarked: "A group like Danone is obviously one of our industrial treasures and we will of course defend the interests of France." The French government subsequently enacted the "Danone Law" which imposes stricter limitations on company takeovers and also enables France to protect 11 key strategic industries, including defense and select forms of information technology as well as yogurt production and casinos.[27]

Bright Food's 2011 bid to purchase Yoplait once again triggered French concerns at the national level. The Chinese firm offered to buy Yoplait for €1.7 billion (approximately $2.3 billion) competing with offers from other multinational companies including General Mills of the US and Nestlé of Switzerland. In the end, General Mills acquired Yoplait for €800 million (approximately $1.12 billion), despite a bid from Bright Food for over double that amount.[28] According to Sophie Meunier, Co-Director of Princeton University's European Union Program: "Selecting General Mills over Bright Food was clearly not done on the basis of simply who offered the most money – Bright Food was the highest bidder. But despite earlier hysteria about the potential American takeover of Danone in 2005, by 2011 the French public (and government) greeted the news that an American company was now the proud owner of Yoplait with a collective sigh of relief. Compared with the specter of Chinese ownership, American ownership was clearly a lesser evil."[29]

Economic patriotism towards a country's long-established corporations is not unique to France, yet it remains perplexing for many onlookers. Several years prior to General Mills' successful acquisition of Yoplait, the prime minister himself remarked that he would "defend the interests of France" against an American firm buying a French dairy company. Why were French officials suddenly ready to accept American ownership of Yoplait, especially given Bright Food's substantially higher offer? One possible explanation is that since its market-leading dairy giant Danone remained under French ownership, a foreign buyer for Yoplait was a viable option. While American firms were not beloved by the French, US-based multinational corporations had overcome the liability of foreignness through decades of international business experience and interaction. Chinese firms, on the other hand, were just getting started. Concerns also existed that perhaps Bright Food would not comply with French labor laws or maybe it would just take the yogurt-producing technology and relocate operations back to China. Beyond the political considerations on the table, there were too many unknowns to judge whether Bright Food's investment would yield a positive economic impact for France.

Since Bright Food's bid for Yoplait ultimately proved unsuccessful, it is unclear whether it would have resulted in a negative outcome for the French yogurt firm. However, this example clearly illustrates how many countries in the West remain wary of the potential economic challenges posed by Chinese investment. They fear unfair labor practices and potential intellectual property theft, discussed in further detail below. In addition, they fear Chinese SOEs in strategic industries will be unfairly subsidized both at home and overseas, making it difficult for Western companies to compete. Politicians argue for "economic reciprocity," the idea that Chinese investment should not be allowed within their nation's borders unless China makes its domestic market more open to Western firms and stops providing preferential procurement policies to Chinese firms. The WTO has become an important framework for US and European countries to press their claims against Chinese international investment and trade practices. Of the 31 disputes China has been directly involved in, 22 were put forth by the US and EU.[30] The EU in particular files a staggering number of cases against Chinese firms related to anti-dumping concerns.

Perhaps the most frequently cited concern in the debate over the economic implications of Chinese investment is intellectual property theft. Intellectual property (IP) theft is one area for concern that is justified based on existing evidence. However, developed legal institutions and oversight mechanisms can prevent industrial espionage. For example, in 2013, the US Justice Department filed criminal charges against one of Goldwind's competitors, Sinovel. According to the *Wall Street Journal*, the Chinese wind turbine firm was charged with multiple violations of corporate espionage law, including "trade-secret theft, criminal copyright infringement and wire fraud." Sinovel shut down four of its overseas subsidiaries following the charges.[31] According to a widely publicized report by the US Intellectual Property Commission, co-chaired by former US ambassador to China Jon M. Huntsman, Jr., China is thought to be behind more than 50 percent of intellectual property theft in the US. The report, which also lists Russia and India as top offenders, estimates that IP theft costs US business as much as $300 billion each year. The report finds that IP theft from China is the most prevalent among Western companies operating in China itself, due to the difficulty in securing technology across long supply chains.[32] To prevent unintended technology transfer, the onus is on both governments and firms. It is essential for governments to enact effective laws with stiff penalties to discourage such cases from occurring, as well as for companies to ensure their internal procedures for preventing IP theft are fully up to date.

Social concerns

The third area of concern related to Chinese investment in the West is its potential negative social impact. "We hope that this successful example of collaboration between Greece and China will encourage more Chinese to come to Greece," Greek President Karolos Papoulias told the media during a May 2013 visit to the port of Piraeus.[33] While Chinese investment in Europe has focused heavily on Germany, France, and the UK, Chinese firms have also invested in distressed states like Greece. The port of Piraeus is one of China's largest investments in Europe. In 2010, state-owned China Ocean Shipping Company (COSCO) leased half of Greece's largest port for an estimated $647 million (500 million euros) for a 35-year period.[34] Depending on who you ask, COSCO's investment is either an economic miracle or a labor rights disaster.

Sophie Meunier, of Princeton's European Union Program, remarks: "COSCO's investment in the port of Piraeus is the most visible and egregious example of the potential negative impact foreign investment by a Chinese firm can have."[35] Prior to signing the deal for the port, COSCO executives reportedly negotiated with the Greek government to fire all unionized workers and then re-hire only non-union members. According to a *New York Times* investigative report, prior to the COSCO takeover some workers made as much as $181,000 a year with overtime, but afterward COSCO paid its Greek workers an average annual salary of less than $23,000. A representative from the Greek Dockworkers' Union remarked that COSCO's investment was "bringing third-world labor standards to Europe," as he described the Chinese firm's poor labor standards and lax quality controls.[36] Lax government policies in nations like Greece and Central European countries do not sufficiently restrict Chinese firms from importing suboptimal business practices as politicians balance a tough stance on these issues with the need to attract Chinese investment for their economic development.

> Chinese businesses operating in the West are local entities and are thus legally bound by the same regulations as domestic firms.

In advanced economies in the West with developed legal institutions and stringent regulations, such as the US, Canada, Australia, and many EU member states, such social violations occur far less frequently. Chinese food producer Shuanghui International's acquisition of US-based Smithfield Foods illustrates the effectiveness of having established regulatory procedures to prevent potentially harmful business practices from occurring in a Western nation. The announcement that a Chinese firm was acquiring Smithfield Foods, an American pork producer, led to immediate public outcry about food safety concerns. The US Food and Drug Administration (FDA) and US Department of Agriculture (USDA) are influential regulatory bodies charged with making sure US citizens are eating safe food. While Shuanghui has a corporate responsibility to produce high-quality products, there is also final responsibility by the US government regulators to make sure only safe food products are stocked on American store shelves. Strong domestic rule of law and regulatory agencies are a central means to ensure Chinese and other foreign companies operate according to the standards of the domestic economy.

Minimizing the potential negative social impact of Chinese investment is an important responsibility for host governments, because Chinese businesses overseas are local entities and are thus legally bound by their regulations. It is up to the recipient government to have the right laws and enforcement mechanisms in place to protect against unfair business practices that could result in negative outcomes for workers, consumers, or the environment.

Key takeaways from this chapter

There are legitimate concerns that arise from Chinese investment in the West; however, as the next chapter discusses, there are significant potential benefits as well. While most Chinese investments go through without any difficulties, the challenges faced by a handful of high-profile deals, primarily in the US, have sent mixed messages to Chinese investors. At the same time, they have provided the media and politicians in China and the West with ample ammunition to paint an inaccurate picture of the current investment environment. Such reports lead the general public in the West to fear rather than welcome Chinese investment. The truth is, the window to Chinese investment is open, but 'holes' remain in existing regulatory screens, which may still allow potential national security and anti-competitive risks. By adopting the proposed solutions in Chapter 8, governments in the West will be better able to maximize the benefits associated with Chinese investment and ensure that any blocked deals are the result of effective, clear, and consistent screening processes rather than unfounded political xenophobia.

chapter 7

The Opportunity: How Can the West Benefit from Chinese Investment?

When Robert J. Remenar was asked his feelings about a Chinese company acquiring his firm Nexteer, he responded: "We were the ones who sought out Chinese investment to begin with." A Michigan-based automotive steering firm, Nexteer was on the verge of collapse until it was acquired by Chinese state-owned AVIC Automobile in 2010. After losing millions of dollars, Nexteer had been spun off from Delphi in 2009. During the global financial crisis, Nexteer found itself under temporary ownership by General Motors (GM); however, Remenar recommended to his management that Nexteer remain "for sale" and not be further integrated into GM. This was because many of Nexteer's clients were GM's competitors, constituting a conflict of interest and forcing Nexteer to continue looking for new owners.

Remenar believed the best option for Nexteer was to find a Chinese buyer. A Chinese acquisition was his preferred path because he felt that a Chinese company would have sufficient capital to invest in his business, would be more long-term oriented than a private equity (PE) firm, and would not further consolidate the automotive steering industry. A private equity firm would take a much more active approach to managing Nexteer, and prepare for a short- to medium-term exit either via acquisition or public listing. Based on his research, Remenar had the impression that Chinese buyers prefer to invest for the long term and to interfere less with existing management given their limited experience operating overseas. Remenar envisioned a best-case scenario in which a Chinese firm would inject a round of capital into Nexteer and interfere with the business as little as possible. That is exactly what happened after AVIC bought Nexteer for $465 million in 2010.[1]

Remenar recounts a speech he gave to Nexteer's employees one year after the acquisition by AVIC. "One year ago people were worried that work was going to be outsourced to China. Not one job moved. People worried that future investment would all be made in China. In that year we invested over $200 million dollars, $100 million of which went to the US, with the remaining amount going predominantly outside of China. Lastly, employees feared that a new Chinese management team would swoop in and run the business. One year later I still had the same exact management team." AVIC's investment in Nexteer preserved approximately 10,000 jobs globally (including 4,000 American jobs), boosted tax revenues for the state of Michigan, and built a bridge to the world's largest automotive market in China. The Nexteer acquisition is an example of an ideal situation in which a struggling Western corporation identifies a complementary Chinese acquirer to breathe life back into its business.[2]

How can the West benefit from Chinese investment?

The potential benefit of Chinese investment may be greatest for markets in the US and EU with struggling companies in need of financial support and economies hungry for job creation and increased tax revenues. While the potential benefits of Chinese investment outlined in this chapter are primarily economic in nature, there are several political and social benefits as well (Table 7.1).

Economic benefits

The economic benefits of Chinese investment are tangible. Governments can easily see quantifiable benefits like employment generation,

Table 7.1　Benefits of Chinese investment in the West

Economic	Social	Political
New jobs & tax revenues	Consumer choice	Interdependence
Revive struggling companies & industries	Global corporate social responsibility practices	
Improved infrastructure		
New market access		

improved sector performance, and increased tax revenues. At the same time, workers at firms previously on the verge of bankruptcy may retain employment under new Chinese ownership. The infrastructure necessary to get goods to markets may be improved to facilitate continued or increased economic exchange. A single greenfield investment (a new project built from the ground up) may create hundreds of new jobs both directly and indirectly through engaging local construction companies, advisory firms, and other third parties. The next sections provide examples and data demonstrating the potential benefits of Chinese investment in the West.

Labor market growth

Employment generation is one of the most visible signs of Chinese investment's potential positive impact in the West. According to a study by the World Economic Forum (WEF) analyzing 95 large Chinese companies with international operations, over 80 percent have established programs to develop local employment opportunities in the overseas markets in which they operate.[3] These figures may be even higher for Chinese investments in advanced economies in the West. When a Chinese company purchases a struggling firm like Nexteer or Volvo, it ensures the company continues to operate and retains existing jobs. For example, Geely's purchase of Volvo cars did not just save a long-standing automobile company; it preserved 16,000 local jobs in Sweden.[4] An acquisition maintains jobs in the short term and may even generate more jobs as the company stabilizes and seeks out more local experts to drive growth. The most new jobs come from greenfield investments, in which a

Chinese company sets up a new factory or other operations and hires an entire labor force to run its overseas business.

Chinese investment-led job growth is still in the nascent stages of its development. This is because the percentage of Chinese overseas direct investment in the West is still small relative to other foreign investors with much more experience. Official figures published by the Chinese Ministry of Commerce state that as of 2013 an estimated 1,600 Chinese companies employ approximately 50,000 workers in Europe.[5] According to investment research firm the Rhodium Group, at the end of 2012 approximately 6 million American jobs were the result of foreign direct investment; however, Chinese firms only accounted for 27,000 of these jobs – less than 1 percent. As China's outbound investment flows increase, these figures will shift dramatically in the future. If the current trajectory of Chinese investment in the US continues, employment generation associated with its firms is projected to increase to as many as 400,000 American jobs by 2020, according to Rhodium.[6]

Yet the job growth statistics associated with Chinese investment in the West only tell part of the story. When a Chinese company like AVIC Automobile invests in the US or EU, it may indirectly fuel job growth in addition to the number of employees it hires directly. First, AVIC may hire an international or local advisory firm to assess which markets outside of China are most suitable for investment given AVIC's unique business and product portfolio. Once AVIC decides to invest in a country such as Germany or the US, it may hire a German or American investment bank to source potential acquisition targets. And once the foreign acquisition target is identified, AVIC may require the services of a host of advisors ranging from tax to legal to public relations to execute the deal. Even after AVIC successfully acquires the foreign firm, it may need construction and engineering firms to improve existing operations and build new facilities. The net impact of AVIC's investment on the local labor market may extend far beyond the local employees it hires.

The economic benefits of Chinese investment are tangible.

Improved infrastructure

Unlike the newly built metropolises found in China's first-tier cities, many aging urban centers across the Western world are in dire need of repair. Crumbling roads, bridges, airports, subways, and ports may require increased investment to operate more safely and efficiently. According to the American Society of Civil Engineers' 2013 *Report Card for America's Infrastructure*, the US needs $3.6 trillion by 2020 to bring its infrastructure up to its own national standards.[7] In his 2014 budget proposal, President Obama called for $50 billion to be spent on US highways and $40 billion on long-distance railways. Chinese investment represents one way to close this gap between pledged and needed funds.[8]

During an April 2013 trip to Beijing, US Secretary of State John Kerry opened his arms to Chinese investment in American infrastructure. He explained: "We have huge infrastructure needs in the United States for a certain series of projects like water projects, transportation projects, energy projects ... It's a win-win-win. It's a win for the investors, it's a win for the countries, and ultimately it's a win for the place where the infrastructure gets built."[9] Kerry knew from his terms as Massachusetts senator about the benefits of Chinese infrastructure investment in the US. In 2002, Danish shipping giant Maersk Line ended its service to the Port of Boston, putting 9,000 local jobs at risk. Later that year, Chinese firm China Ocean Shipping (Group) Company (COSCO) opened a direct service from China to Boston, not only saving these 9,000 jobs, but creating an additional 7,000 jobs within a year. Ten years after COSCO's initial investment, the Massachusetts Port Authority's CEO praised the firm for preserving more than 34,000 local jobs in the decade following its investment.[10] COSCO's investment in Boston also demonstrates how Chinese investment operating under a sound regulatory environment can minimize the potential negative impact on local labor conditions – as compared with COSCO's controversial investment in the Port of Piraeus in a more loosely regulated Greek market.

Giving Western companies a second chance

Qu Xiangjun, an executive at major machine tool manufacturer Beijing Number One, strolls the quaint streets of a picturesque small town – Coburg in Germany. When asked by a German reporter why his firm would invest in such an isolated area, he replied: *maque sui xiao, wuzang juquan* (麻雀虽小, 五脏俱全) translating as, "a sparrow may be small, but it still has all of its vital organs." Qu believed that despite its small size, Coburg possessed all of the necessary attributes for his firm's 2005 investment in then-struggling German industrial machinery firm Waldrich Coburg.[11]

Founded in 1920, Waldrich was most recently owned by American firm Ingersoll International. After Ingersoll filed for bankruptcy in the US in 2003, Waldrich turned to a long-time customer to come to its aid. Beijing Number One, a subsidiary of state-owned Jingcheng Holding, had become a Waldrich customer in 1984, more than 20 years prior to the initial conversations about purchasing the German firm. Beijing Number One's 2005 purchase of Waldrich made it the Chinese firm's first overseas acquisition. The preexisting long-term relationship between Waldrich and Beijing Number One, combined with the Chinese senior management's strong commitment that no significant changes to operations would be made, helped the acquisition to go through smoothly.

Before long, signs reflecting the strength of the acquisition began to appear. After its first year under Chinese ownership, Waldrich's profits increased by over fifty percent. By 2010, its annual revenues doubled to €170 million (approximately $225 million). The same management team and number of local employees remained following the acquisition, with one Chinese executive and 250 new employees added to the original 500. Much of the firm's success was driven by the effective implementation of a dual-brand strategy under which high-end products were marketed under the Waldrich Coburg name, while lower-end products used the Beijing Number One name. This approach was not dissimilar from that employed by Pearl River Piano with its separate high-end Ritmüller brand discussed in Chapter 4. Beijing Number One also helped Waldrich win more business with a wide range of new Chinese industrial firm customers. Like the Nexteer case in the US, Chinese investment gave Waldrich a second chance.[12]

In the wake of the global financial crisis, there are more companies in the West like Nexteer and Waldrich that need new owners to stay afloat. Injection of capital occurs primarily through one of two methods: private equity (PE) ownership or a corporate acquisition. PE-ownership may appear to be an attractive approach, but it presents a number of challenges for the company being purchased. According to Jack Perkowski, Managing Partner of JFP Holdings and author of *Managing the Dragon*: "The CEO, formerly the top decision-maker in the company, now answers to the representative assigned from the private equity firm. Not only does the American or European firm lose managerial autonomy, it also risks focusing too much on short-term results due to the private equity firm's top goal of maximizing its investment."[13] Chinese ownership may be a good alternative to private equity because it is likely to be more hands-off in the management of day-to-day business. It may even be in a position to reinvest more after its first round of investment, which would be almost unheard of under private equity ownership. However, it is important to recognize that what might start off as a "hands-off" approach may become more direct in the future. This does not necessarily mean that after a few years a Chinese firm will fire local employees or relocate factories to China. But, as Chinese owners gain experience and confidence operating in the overseas market, they may begin to take a more active role in managing the business – from selecting leadership positions to determining new areas of business expansion.

Breathing life into struggling sectors

The shift of labor-intensive manufacturing to China devastated America's manufacturing sector in the 1980s and 1990s. The Boston Consulting Group (BCG) estimates the US lost 6 million manufacturing jobs as a result of China's emergence as "the world's factory."[14] Now, as American high-tech manufacturing is rebounding, Chinese firms are playing an important role in the revival of US firms. John Ling is helping to make this possible. Ling is technically based in Shanghai, where he serves as the China Managing Director for the South Carolina Department of

Commerce, one of over 30 US state trade representative offices located in Shanghai. He is busy these days traveling between the US and China on a monthly basis to educate Chinese investors about the potential business opportunities for their firms in South Carolina. John is a sea turtle, originally from China; however, he left China for the US in 1991 to finish his MBA at Charleston Southern University. After graduation, he stayed in the US where he co-founded a business exporting preengineered metal buildings to China. The buildings were produced in Houston, Texas, and Ling's firm exported them to a range of Chinese industrial companies.

After five years in business, Ling was referred to a business contact at Haier, a Chinese home appliances firm. Haier was in the process of determining whether to set up its new US production facility in Florida or Connecticut. Given the manufacturing capabilities Haier would need for the facility, John recommended that they consider South Carolina.[15] After a short visit, the management team did not take long to change their minds. In 1999, they announced a $30 million investment in Camden, South Carolina, that was increased to $60 million in 2006.[16] Haier's investment is only one of many Chinese manufacturing investments in the US. From Sany's $60 million[17] industrial equipment manufacturing facility in Peachtree, Georgia; to Golden Dragon Precise Copper Tube Group's planned $100 million[18] plant in Thomasville, Alabama; to Tianjin Pipe's $1 billion[19] steel pipe factory in Corpus Christi, Texas – Chinese investments in American manufacturing are on the rise.

As Chapter 2 explains, the primary business motivations for Chinese companies to go global are to gain access to markets, new capabilities (especially technology) and global brands. By producing in the US, Chinese companies' goods are closer to a key market, allowing them to adjust manufacturing capacity more effectively for their North American customers. Additionally, Chinese firms secure advanced production technologies operated by a highly productive workforce. A report on the US manufacturing industry by BCG concludes that the high productivity of the American workforce makes manufacturing in the US relatively more profitable than China where labor, energy, and real estate costs all continue to rise.[20] M&A and greenfield investments in America's manufacturing sector allow Chinese firms to achieve their commercial aims, while fueling the next era of US manufacturing.

Access to new markets in China

Chinese investment not only has potential to buoy Western companies and industries, it may also open new market opportunities in China for acquired Western firms. The wine industry is flourishing in China and the nation is set to overtake the US as the largest consumer of wine by 2015, according to UK data provider Euromonitor International. COFCO Wine & Spirits, the beverage division of Chinese state-owned food conglomerate China National Cereals, Oils and Foodstuffs Corp (COFCO), intends to capitalize on Chinese consumers' evolving palate. COFCO has historically marketed only domestically produced wines under its flagship Great Wall brand, but in a 2013 interview Shu Yu, a senior manager for the firm, informed reporters: "We will announce that Great Wall is not only from China, and we will make a French Great Wall, a Chilean Great Wall and an Australian Great Wall."[21]

COFCO's overseas wine supplies originate from a series of strategic acquisitions. In 2010 COFCO purchased Chile's Bisquertt Vineyard for $18 million. One year later, it paid €10 million (approximately $13 million) for French vineyard, Château de Viaud in Lalande de Pomerol. In 2013, COFCO senior management announced that their firm plans to acquire a vineyard in the Barossa Valley region of Australia. Through its overseas acquisition strategy, COFCO is satisfying a demand for imported wine in China that is growing at an estimated 20% per year. The tremendous growth of the Chinese wine market has had a positive impact on the earnings and employment levels of the acquired vineyards. According to a 2013 report by the *New York Times*, the wine industry employs approximately 500,000 people in France. Roughly 20,000 of these jobs are currently supported by sales to China.[22] In short, the West has much to gain economically from new market access in China.

> Chinese investment not only has potential to buoy Western companies and industries, it may also open new market opportunities in China.

Social benefits

Does increased investment make Chinese companies act "more like us" over the long term? Some scholars of foreign investment argue that the longer Chinese companies operate in North America, EU, and Australia under more stringent regulatory conditions, the higher the likelihood that they will adopt business practices induced by compliance to Western standards as their global business practice in other markets in which they operate. They argue that as a company like Huawei competes fairly in the US market, selling its mobile devices under American regulatory standards, it will be more likely to implement similar practices related to fair pricing strategy and labor conditions in other developed and developing markets. It is difficult to prove whether ultimately this will be the case, but evidence demonstrates that corporate social responsibility practices among global Chinese firms are on the rise. According to the World Economic Forum study titled *Emerging Best Practices of Chinese Globalizers*, Chinese corporations are taking Corporate Social Responsibility (CSR) more seriously by choice and due to heightened pressure from regulators and international society.[23]

In 2013, China's Ministry of Commerce (MOFCOM) in conjunction with the Ministry of Environmental Protection (MEP) released a set of guidelines for Chinese companies investing overseas. The *Guidelines on Environmental Protection for China's Outbound Investment and Cooperation* (对外投资合作环境保护指南) are intended to promote the adoption of global CSR practices in the host countries where Chinese firms operate internationally.[24]

The guidelines cover the following eight areas (Table 7.2):

Table 7.2   MOFCOM–MEP guidelines for corporate social responsibility

1.	Respect for local culture
2.	Local community development
3.	Labor rights protection (environmental, health and safety standards)
4.	Bio-diversity management
5.	Environmental conservation
6.	Green procurement
7.	Partner with local communities on their sustainability agenda
8.	Adopt international best practices for CSR

While following these guidelines from MOFCOM and the MEP is not mandatory, Chinese companies investing in the West face pressure from multiple additional sources to improve their practices. First and most importantly, Chinese firms face pressure from stakeholders within the host nation to ensure their business practices are not detrimental to local societies. Reports by international media and organizations such as Human Rights Watch have greatly increased scrutiny of Chinese firms' activities overseas. In addition, there is "soft power" pressure from the Chinese government, which aims to ensure the actions of its companies operating in the West reflect well on how China as a country is perceived by the world. In addition to the guidelines above, the Ministry of Foreign Affairs (MFA) has also joined the United Nations Global Compact, a policy initiative calling on businesses to implement a series of principles related to human rights, labor, environment, and anti-corruption in their business operations.[25]

Lenovo and Haier are two Chinese companies that are already making concerted and systematic efforts to reduce their environmental impact. Lenovo implemented a product "end-of-life" initiative to recycle outdated Lenovo personal computers across 50 countries. In its first five years, this initiative generated over 28,000 tons of recycled materials for Lenovo computer production. Meanwhile, Haier formed a global research and development alliance with US-based Dow Chemical and seven other global companies to develop green technology solutions for the consumer electronics industry. The focus of the alliance is to reduce chlorofluorocarbon emissions from consumer electronics that contribute to ozone depletion. As two of the more experienced Chinese firms operating in overseas markets, Lenovo and Haier serve as good examples for less experienced Chinese firms entering Western markets for the first time.[26]

Corporate philanthropy among global Chinese firms is also improving. This is not to say that all Chinese companies operating in the West are donating money, volunteer time and other forms of philanthropic support to local communities where they invest – in fact, very few firms do so. However, there are notable examples of selected Chinese firms that have given back to Western society. For example, Wang Jianlin's Wanda supported the local community in Kansas City, where AMC Entertainment was based, following its acquisition of the American movie theater chain. Wanda donated $1.3 million worth of goods and services to local high schools.[27] Wind turbine producer, Goldwind, donated €500,000 (approximately $650,000) to Germany's Saarland University to support alternative energy education.[28] These are just a few examples of what will hopefully be more corporate philanthropy from Chinese firms operating in Western markets in the future.

Political benefits

Do healthy business relations lead to peaceful political relations?

International relations scholars have debated for years whether a link exists between increased economic interdependence and improved political relations. Within the liberal paradigm in international relations theory, some argue that increased interdependence raises the costs of conflict between nations, thereby leading to greater cooperation. Other scholars point out that increased economic interchange can also lead to greater friction between countries, and they note that strategic factors are likely to trump economic interdependence in decisions of war or peace.

Tom Wright, a Research Fellow at the Brookings Institution, argues that we need to differentiate between "good interdependence" and "bad interdependence." According to Wright's definition, good interdependence produces stability from trade, foreign investment, and educational exchanges. On the other hand, bad interdependence can lead to instability resulting from financial imbalances, corporate espionage, or energy insecurity. Despite the challenges of interdependence, there is potential for the "good" interdependence to outweigh the "bad" and for Chinese investment to promote a more mutually beneficial political relationship between China and Western nations.[29] From AVIC's successful investment in Nexteer, Nexteer's employees, local government officials, and the citizens of Saginaw, Michigan, have seen the potential upside of Chinese investment and their views are no longer purely shaped by headlines about the latest troubled Chinese investment or politicians' rhetoric. This increased mutual understanding and mutual economic benefit in and of itself is a positive result of increased interdependence.

Key takeaways from this chapter

As long as appropriate and effective regulatory systems are in place to protect national security and fair competition, Chinese investment can benefit the West's economic, social, and political interests. Chinese investment saves existing jobs and may even add new ones. In addition to aiding struggling companies, Chinese firms can help breathe life into entire industries, like manufacturing. As companies operating under Western business law, Chinese firms contribute valuable tax dollars that can be used to fuel the local economy. They can also invest to rebuild aging infrastructure and implement more efficient road, rail, air, and shipping channels to power economic activity. There is growing evidence suggesting that as Chinese companies invest responsibly in the West, there are also social benefits related to environmental, educational, and cultural initiatives. The potential benefits of increased Chinese investment in the West are tremendous, and it is in the interests of Western governments to make the most of this opportunity.

Part **IV**

The Response

chapter 8

The Response: Maximizing Benefits, Minimizing Concerns

Are Chinese companies' investments in the West a good thing? Unfortunately, it takes more than a simple "yes" or "no" to answer this question. The West has much to gain from the global emergence of Chinese companies, including more jobs, tax revenues, improved infrastructure, and new market access. However, there are valid reasons why Chinese investments should not all be welcomed, such as concerns about national security, cyber-security, and anti-competitiveness. Targeted efforts must be made to ensure that Chinese investment in the West is mutually beneficial at the government, corporate, and individual levels. This chapter provides practical recommendations about how the West and China should both respond in the years and decades ahead to maximize the benefits of Chinese investment while minimizing concerns.

In May 2011, the Asia Society, a non-profit organization promoting mutual understanding between Asia and the U.S., released a report titled *An American Open Door? Maximizing the Benefits of Chinese Foreign Direct Investment*.[1] The report's recommendations are directed toward the American government's response but are highly applicable to other Western nations within the context of their respective political, social, and economic spheres. Building on the Asia Society's government-focused recommendations, the following sections provide further guidance to

Table 8.1 Recommendations for the West

Political	Companies	Social
• Clearly state the areas in which Chinese investment is welcome • Implement an objective framework for threat assessment • Remove politics from investment review to the greatest possible extent • Systematize and coordinate the promotion of Chinese investment at national and local levels	• Ensure fair play among competitors • Consider industry impact when forming partnerships • Assess the viability of Chinese ownership through M&A	• Increase cross-cultural education to bridge the "trust gap" across all parties

Western and Chinese corporations about how they should also respond (Table 8.1).

Recommendations for Western governments

Clearly state the areas in which Chinese investment is welcome

Executives in China receive mixed messages about Western attitudes toward Chinese investment. On one hand, they hear about peers that have successfully entered Western markets, like Lenovo and Wanxiang. On the other hand, controversial deals like those discussed in Chapter 6 send a different message, prompting Chinese executives to think: "Maybe the West isn't as open to foreign investment as commercial trade representatives lead us to believe?" Western nations need to clearly articulate the sectors in which foreign investment is welcome, the review process for how proposed investments will be assessed, and how the review process will be separated from politicians seeking to use an anti-China stance for political gain.

Arthur Kroeber of consulting firm GaveKal Dragonomics explains his findings from research on foreign investment deals in Australia in Chapter 6.

Even though the data clearly revealed that Chinese investment was in fact welcome in Australia, the Chinese executives he encountered still felt the market was not open to Chinese investment. Kroeber attributes this misperception about Western investment climates to attention focused on a "very small number of cases that appeared politically motivated and were obsessively discussed both in Beijing and Washington."[2] How can the West minimize the number of proposed investments that develop into these controversial incidents, to ensure that it benefits from Chinese investment?

Regard each deal as unique

As discussed in Chapter 7, Tom Wright of the Brookings Institution argues that there is both "good" and "bad" interdependence. He suggests that a nation should create protected sectors of its economy to provide guidance to Chinese and other foreign investors about which areas of the economy are open to foreign investment. However, such an approach may not be possible to implement in the current global business environment. For example, the U.S. could not open its telecommunications industry to foreign investment from Alcatel-Lucent and Ericsson, but close this sector for Chinese companies like Huawei and ZTE. Similarly, France could not keep American investment out of its dairy industry by blocking PepsiCo's acquisition of Danone, while allowing General Mills to acquire Yoplait just a few years later (see Chapter 6). The key for Western governments is to implement an objective foreign investment review process to assess individual deals as they emerge. At the same time, Western nations also need to consider the unique concerns raised by each deal.

Implement an effective framework for threat assessment

The national security review process for foreign investment should strive to be clear, consistent, and effective. As a first step, Western governments should critically assess their current national security review process with reference to an objective framework. The *Framework for Threat Assessment* by Theodore Moran of the Peterson Institute for International

Economics is one possible option.[3] Moran's assessment method does not discriminate on the basis of an investor's nationality. It provides an objective approach to determine whether or not a potential acquisition poses a threat to national security. Applying this method to the evaluation of Chinese acquisitions of Western firms highlights three categories of relevant threats:

- **Threat 1:** The economy of the Western nation where the Chinese acquisition takes place becomes overly dependent on the Chinese firm for supplies of critical goods and services in a certain industry.
- **Threat 2:** Technology or skills are transferred to the Chinese firm that could be deployed by the Chinese firm or Chinese government in a manner that is harmful to the national interest of the Western nation where the acquisition takes place.
- **Threat 3:** Capability for infiltration, surveillance, or sabotage in the Western nation where the acquisition takes place is created as a result of Chinese investment.

The process relies on determining whether a Chinese (or any foreign) acquisition poses a threat to a Western nation. The first step, defined as the "criticality test," assesses each of the three threats above to determine their applicability to the proposed acquisition. Acquisitions that pose little to no threat are allowed to pass without further national security review. Acquisitions that potentially pose greater threats move on to step two, the "plausible threat test." The plausible threat test assesses the availability of alternative global suppliers and the ease of switching from the current supplier to a new one. If there are many other global suppliers and it is relatively easy to switch to alternative suppliers, then the acquisition is allowed. The last step is directed specifically at Western firms on the brink of bankruptcy that may fail without a foreign acquisition despite the fact that this might lead to further consolidation in the industry. Under this circumstance, the foreign acquisition may be blocked if it is determined that the Western firm is capable of becoming or remaining internationally competitive through its own efforts or support from alternative domestic investors. Under extreme circumstances where the Western firm has no alternative to regain its competitiveness and the Chinese firm is a "buyer of last resort", the Chinese firm may still be allowed to proceed with its acquisition depending on the circumstances.

Figure 8.1 illustrates the framework for threat assessment applied to a Chinese acquisition of a Western company.

To understand the framework in practice, take the fictitious example of an attempted acquisition of French telecommunications firm France-Co by China-Co. French regulators would first apply the criticality test to determine if any of the three threats apply and to what extent. The next step would be to determine if there are other more suitable investor alternatives beyond China-Co. For example, if US-based US-Co bids to takeover France-Co, or a European private equity firm decides to provide needed capital to France-Co, then the French government might block China-Co's proposed acquisition. But if there are no suitable alternative investors – and the French review process determines that France-Co faces potential bankruptcy without external investment and that China-Co's acquisition would not further consolidate the telecommunications industry – then it might allow the deal to go through.

Moran discusses the example of Lenovo's acquisition of IBM's PC business:

> Might the Lenovo acquisition represent a worrisome outflow of tightly held capabilities to China? Competition among personal computer producers is sufficiently intense that basic production technology is considered commoditized: more than a dozen producers compete for fifty percent of the PC market, with no one showing a predominant edge for long. PC assembly is much less concentrated than some hardware or software components... It is farfetched to think that Lenovo's acquisition of IBM's PC business represented a leakage of sensitive technology, or provided China with military-application or dual-use capabilities that are not readily available elsewhere.[4]

Western governments should adopt a consistent and objective approach to assess the national security concerns posed by foreign direct investment. The framework for threat assessment provides the basis for a model

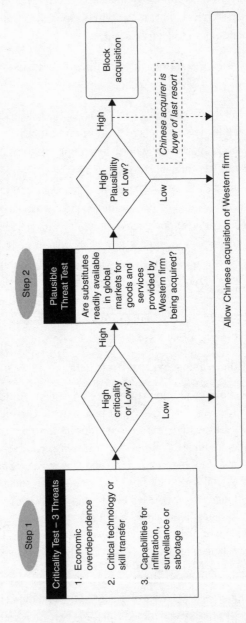

FIGURE 8.1 Should a Chinese acquisition of a Western firm be allowed or blocked?

Source: Author's own image based on Moran, Theodore. "Foreign Acquisitions and National Security": December 2009.

that can be implemented across countries and executed in a clear and standardized manner when assessing a potential acquisition by Chinese or other foreign buyers.

Remove politics from investment review to the greatest possible extent

Chapter 6 introduced legitimate concerns explaining why not all Chinese investment should be welcomed. That chapter also quoted the words of Chinese economic reformer Deng Xiaoping, "when you open a window, fresh air will come in, but so will some flies," recognizing that not all investment from foreign investors is beneficial. Building on the basis of an objective framework for threat assessment will create an effective investment review screen letting in welcome investment while keeping out potentially threatening deals. Yet the best-designed foreign investment assessment approach can fail if the wrong voices have a say at the review table.

At the time of writing this book, Chinese state-owned Shuanghui International has just acquired American pork producer Smithfield Foods. Shuanghui's record-breaking $4.7 billion investment gives it complete ownership of the American pork producer.[5] But before CFIUS scrutiny of the deal even began, politicians started to appear on major news networks such as CNN and FOX News expressing their "concerns" about food safety and product quality. As alluded to in Chapter 6, many of the politicians have no stake in the business outcome, but rather are out to take a hard stance against China to win favor with local voters. No one took into consideration the fact that after the acquisition, a Shuanghui-owned Smithfield Foods would not receive any special treatment and would be subject to the same regulatory standards and oversight as domestic firms. If poor-quality pork entered American households, it would be regulatory bodies like the Food and Drug Administration (FDA) or the US Department of Agriculture (USDA) on the chopping block – not just the Chinese owners of Smithfield.

The ongoing politicization of high-profile Chinese investments perpetuates the myth that Chinese investment is not welcome in the West. This is contrary to what the data actually reveals. The data shows that the vast majority of attempted Chinese investments are successfully completed without government interference. But if such misleading rhetoric continues, Chinese firms will choose to invest where they feel most confident that their investments will go through both smoothly and successfully. Western nations seen by Chinese firms as "unwelcome to Chinese investment" as a result of unclear, inconsistently applied, or politically motivated regulatory procedures will miss a tremendous opportunity to benefit from Chinese investment.

> The ongoing politicization of high-profile Chinese investments perpetuates the myth that Chinese investment is not welcome in the West.

Consider political priorities, focus on economic factors

With a defined process in place to evaluate potential national security threats, Western nations should focus on economic factors and communicate from the senior government level down that Chinese investment is welcome.[6] This message should begin with an official statement, but should also be reinforced by trade dialogues, bilateral forums and on the Internet. This message needs to be targeted toward the relevant Chinese investors for a particular industry or location of investment. It should also be made as accessible as possible by choosing the appropriate channels to deliver the message. For example many Chinese businesspeople may feel more comfortable conducting research online and chatting informally through one-on-one internet messaging tools rather than attending a live Q&A session. It is critical that all communications are in Mandarin and local languages – leave no room for misinterpretation. The message should be clear, consistent, and repeated regularly to strengthen bilateral communication on investment issues. At the same time, these communications by Western governments will help to provide a more objective economic context for any domestic voices that might focus solely on political factors.

Systematize and coordinate the promotion of Chinese investment at national and local levels

Chinese executives may want their firms to expand into developed markets, but they are not sure which national or local actors to turn to for information and advice. Within the Chinese business environment, they are accustomed to turning to relevant government bodies as their first resource for business guidance. They may expect a Western equivalent to China's *Catalogue for Guidance for Foreign Investment* (外商投资产业指导目录), a periodically updated guide outlining encouraged foreign investment projects in China and published by the National Development and Reform Commission. However, in most developed Western economies, governments tend to be much more hands off when it comes to business. To maximize the potential benefits of Chinese investment, Western governments should take a more proactive approach at the national, provincial, and local levels. The approach should be systematized with clear roles for governments at each level. It should also provide Chinese investors with detailed information about the relevant regulations and incentives for investment in certain regions. Without effective coordination and communication, Chinese investors may be confused about investment procedures, and investment itself will travel opportunistically among national or sub-national locations.

Improve data accessibility

One of the primary concerns Western businesses have about investing in China is the accessibility and reliability of government-supplied data. From high-level statistics such as GDP forecasts down to granular city performance data, Western governments and businesses remain skeptical of officially reported figures. Instead, they choose to rely on specialized third-party data providers and consultants to supply what they believe to be more accurate information. However, unlike most data reported from within China, which remains under a shroud of suspicion, Chinese overseas investment can be clearly quantified if recipient governments adopt a coordinated approach to data collection. For example, several investment recruitment agencies in the

West create "Project Profiles" for proposed investments from China and other overseas investors. The project profile measures the potential net economic impact of an investment to their domestic economy by documenting expected job creation, land and building use, energy consumption, and a range of other factors. Successful investments are documented and tracked by local agencies. If such data were collected and reported in a consistent manner at the state level in the US or even the country level in the EU, then the available dataset would paint a highly accurate picture of the nature and volume of Chinese investment in the West. The resulting data could help indirectly inform Chinese businesses about where they should consider investing based on the industry distribution of the already documented investment cases. Meanwhile, the dataset could serve as a valuable means to encourage greater cooperation among the various government stakeholders competing for Chinese investment in their respected regions. The following sections further detail how the current uncoordinated approach to investment recruitment adopted by American and European governments has caused them to miss out on maximizing the benefits of Chinese investment.

> Chinese overseas investment can be clearly quantified if recipient governments adopt a coordinated approach to data collection.

Remedy the disconnect between federal and state levels in the US

After the American government sends a clear message to China that the US is truly open for business, it needs to adopt a more unified approach to promoting Chinese investment at the federal and state levels. Currently, the federal government promotes the US through three organizations: SelectUSA (business), BrandUSA (tourism) and EducationUSA (study abroad in the US). The first two organizations are affiliated with the Department of Commerce while the latter is affiliated with the Department of State.

To focus on the specific example of SelectUSA: this organization is charged with promoting the US business environment to foreign investors from around the world. In China, SelectUSA primarily fulfills its mission by traveling to various provinces and hosting events at which Chinese firms interested in investing in the US can learn more about the American business environment. The format for these presentations is typically structured as follows:

- Part I: Case studies of Chinese companies that have successfully entered the US
- Part II: Overview of the advantages of investing in the US
- Part III: Introduction to SelectUSA
- Part IV: Q&A

According to Aaron Brickman, Deputy Executive Director for SelectUSA: "Chinese executives are very interested in learning about investing in the United States. Beyond larger events, I have found that these executives prefer informal meetings as a way of asking their questions and engaging in discussion around their particular topics of interest."[7]

One can only imagine the amount of financial and human resources necessary to meet every Chinese businessperson interested in investing in the US in a one-on-one setting. Yet even in its current format, China's vast size and SelectUSA's full-time China-based staff of six makes it nearly impossible for SelectUSA to hold enough forums to have a meaningful impact. To supplement its live forums, SelectUSA would be wise to learn from Germany's Trade & Invest, the economic development agency of Germany, and create a Chinese language website with a detailed Q&A section addressing common concerns. SelectUSA could also go a step further and use Chinese social media tools such as Weibo, WeChat, and QQ instant messenger to engage with Chinese businesspeople one-on-one to answer their individual questions. This would ensure that the US has a "24-hour storefront" in China. In addition, SelectUSA would gain valuable intelligence about Chinese investors, enabling it to identify common characteristics, concerns, and trends to improve its engagement strategy. A dual online-offline approach is best suited for the current stage where SelectUSA's staffing capacity is simply not sufficient to meet potential Chinese demand across more than 30 provinces.

While SelectUSA is doing the best it can with its limited resources, it is only empowered to deliver one message: "the US welcomes your investment." It is not able to specify or advise potential investors: "this is the specific industry or even this is the state that you should consider investing in." At the same time, a small group of US state governors and city mayors visit China on trade missions to recruit Chinese investment and introduce specific projects in their individual regions. State representatives may partner with one of 33 US state trade offices in China, like the office operated by John Ling of South Carolina from Chapter 7. According to Justin Knapp, Director of Ogilvy Public Relations' China Outbound practice, these trade missions often involve the following elements:[8]

1. Attend the signing of a Memorandum of Understanding ("MOU") between a Chinese SOE and a Western multinational company
2. A stop at one of China's leading universities for a forum often sponsored by a green technology or sustainable development-focused Chinese think-tank
3. American Chamber of Commerce-facilitated meetings and events
4. High-level government-to-government meetings with officials from the Ministry of Commerce (MOFCOM)

This situation clearly illustrates the disconnect between federal and state efforts to promote Chinese investment. Through SelectUSA, the federal government cannot recommend particular industries or locations where Chinese companies should invest. Therefore, the only specific guidance Chinese investors receive is often from state government officials who are traveling to China for trade missions. Such state officials are incentivized to promote their own interests – seeking out job creation and tax dollars that will fuel their local economies. So neither state nor federal representatives can tell Chinese executives what they really want to hear: "We're open for investment. Here is where you should invest. This is the advisor who you should work with on the ground to make it happen." Therefore the only remaining, but often impractical, option is for Chinese firms to send their own exploratory delegations overseas without a clear focus.

The U.S. should bridge this federal-state gap by adopting a more systematic and coordinated approach to promoting investment from Chinese companies. With small trade offices in China, irregular governor visits from some states, and understaffed federal agencies, actors at the state and federal levels should be working together to attract investment and to consistently communicate information about investment regulations and procedures. Instead, in some cases levels are competing with each other, or providing inconsistent information to potential Chinese investors. Chinese firms' interest in investing in the American market is vast and growing; the pie is big enough for everyone to have a fair slice if they work together.

Remedy the disconnect between the European Union and its member states

The situation between the European Union (EU) and the governments of its member states is strikingly similar – if not even more disconnected. EU member states have historically managed their own approaches to attracting and reviewing foreign investment. When the provisions of the Lisbon Treaty aimed at deepening macro-economic coordination went into effect in 2009, the EU gained the power to regulate inbound FDI on behalf of member states. But while the EU now technically has the authority to regulate foreign investment in member states, implementation of a unified regulatory scheme has been difficult to implement in practice. According to research conducted by Sophie Meunier, Co-Director of Princeton University's European Union Program:

> In order to attract Chinese FDI, EU countries are employing a variety of methods which put them in competition with one another. They use national investment promotion agencies. They use national incentives, from taxation to social policies. And sometimes they free-ride by offering very lax, if not non-existent, regulatory conditions for entry... If one of its proposed deals were to be blocked in France or Germany, where FDI in certain sensitive sectors has to be screened, [a Chinese firm] can easily locate its operations in Hungary instead, or another EU country with no FDI restrictions.[9]

Meunier raises a critical point about the difference between the foreign investment environments in the EU compared to the US. Within the 28 member states that comprise the EU, there are 14 countries (primarily in central, eastern, and southern Europe) that currently have no national security review processes. As Meunier's example suggests, when a Chinese company like Huawei faces challenges entering a western European country like France or Germany, it can make the same investment in one of the 14 countries with less stringent regulations – and still gain access to the single EU marketplace. Cleverly exploiting this loophole is unfair in practice, because once a firm is in one of the EU member states, it can circulate its goods freely in the Eurozone market.[10] If a firm manufactures a car in Bulgaria, then it can be sold anywhere, including in the countries that may have rejected the automobile production facility in the first place. EU member states would be wise to tackle the political obstacles to unifying their regulatory framework for the single Eurozone market. As Meunier writes: "The lack of a single voice in investment policy also had a major, self-reinforcing impact on inbound investments: it fostered competition between member states in order to attract foreign investment, especially in the current context of economic crisis in Europe, which could potentially lead to a regulatory race to the bottom."[11]

Like the US, the European Union needs to better coordinate its approach to Chinese inbound investment between the levels of the EU and individual member states. Healthy competition among member states to attract foreign investment is positive; however, if certain states play by a completely different set of rules, then it's not fair for countries with more stringent policies. Chinese companies' ability under the existing legal framework to invest in EU member states with more lax laws and still gain access to the entire EU market precisely illustrates the need for a more unified and systematic approach to attracting and regulating Chinese investment in Europe.

Recommendations for Western companies

As Western governments make the necessary adjustments to encourage mutually beneficial Chinese investment, Western companies will increasingly encounter new Chinese firms operating in their own backyards.

Western firms will need to adjust their business strategies to respond to these new market entrants from the East. Chinese firms entering Western markets may become their new competitors, new partners, or even new owners. Depending on which of these relationships a Western company has with its Chinese counterpart, the response required varies. When competing against Chinese firms within Western markets, domestic companies should work with regulators and industry associations to ensure the Chinese firm is competing fairly and not benefiting from special government incentives, such as preferential access to financing or tax incentives from the Chinese government, which give it an unfair advantage. Western companies seeking to partner with Chinese companies should assess the long-term impact not only on their individual firm, but also on their industry domestically and overseas. Finally, given the weak economic performance of many advanced economies, struggling Western companies should assess the potential advantages and disadvantages of Chinese ownership compared with being acquired by another Western company or a private equity firm.

Chinese companies as competitors: ensure fair play

One key point about Chinese investment is that when a Chinese company operates in a Western market, it must operate in accordance with local regulations and business practices – or else face the consequences. If it is operating as a legal entity in the West, the Chinese firm does not necessarily carry over the poor product quality, food safety, or corrupt business practices that may be prevalent in China. A Chinese company competing within the same legal bounds as other domestic and foreign companies should not be feared or discriminated against. These Chinese firms may benefit the industry as a whole, forcing Western competitors to innovate, ultimately leading to better products and services for customers. However, there may be cases where Chinese firms receive special incentives from the Chinese government (particularly state-owned enterprises), which could enable them to compete at unfair price points or extend contract terms at less than market value to their customers. If a Western government's review process takes into account anti-competitive concerns, such a situation can be avoided. However, Western firms operating within the same industry should remain vigilant and work together to lobby relevant regulators and government bodies to prevent any anti-competitive business practices by foreign investors.

Chinese companies as partners: consider industry impact

Partnerships with Chinese companies can open up access to new international markets, especially in China. In theory, this might sound like an ideal relationship: the Western partners possess technical know-how or a world-class brand, while the Chinese partner brings capital and new market access. But what happens to the industry as a whole when the Chinese partner is able to produce the product on its own? Western companies should consider the long-term implications of partnerships with Chinese firms, in particular the issue of intellectual property or technology transfer.

To cite just one case, Hollywood is now forming partnerships with Chinese production houses at a rapid pace – from animation studio DreamWorks to *Titanic* director James Cameron. While many of their co-produced films will appear on the screens of Dalian Wanda's AMC movie theaters in the US, many will also appear in Wanda-branded theaters in China. As collaboration between Hollywood and Chinese firms deepens over time, it will be interesting to see the impact these partnerships have on the Chinese movie production industry. Will Chinese production houses close the "knowledge gap" and begin producing blockbuster international films of their own? Perhaps Hollywood will not be as welcome in China then, but it's impossible to know for sure. Partnerships with Chinese companies can offer important benefits in the short-term. But Western firms should also consider the long-term impact on their respective industries before their management team says *"gan bei"* and raises glasses of Chinese *baijiu* to toast new partnerships in Beijing.[12]

Chinese companies as owners: it may make sense

Chinese ownership through an acquisition may be a good option for troubled Western firms. In Chapter 7, Robert Remenar, the former CEO of

Nexteer, actively sought out Chinese owners. His firm desperately needed capital investment, but he did not want to operate under more hands-on private equity management, nor did he want to risk an acquisition by a Western competitor. He knew that the fundamentals of Nexteer's business were working well, but its debt prevented the firm from making the investments necessary to improve its competitive position. Chinese ownership through AVIC provided Nexteer with the capital it needed to restart its automotive components business. Also in Chapter 7, Beijing Number One did the same for Waldrich Coburg in Germany. There are likely to be other Western companies that would benefit from Chinese ownership; however, as is the case with any foreign acquisition, Western firms should conduct thorough due diligence to ensure the potential Chinese owners are a good fit.

Regardless of whether Western companies are assessing a new Chinese competitor, partner, or owner, they should treat each situation as a unique case. Given the differences among the types of Chinese firms introduced in Chapter 1, it is unproductive – and even potentially misleading – to group Chinese businesses together instead of evaluating them individually.

Recommendations for Chinese and Western societies

Increase cross-cultural understanding

It is imperative that the citizens of Chinese and Western societies – just as much as the executives of their firms – work toward bridging the "trust gap" discussed in Chapter 2. Some citizens of Western societies perceive Chinese companies as having hidden, potentially malicious, motives driving their commercial behavior. Conversely, some Chinese citizens may believe that the West discriminates against Chinese firms overseas to prevent China from achieving global competitiveness and economically or politically challenging the West. If such egregious generalizations by both sides remain commonplace in the decades to come, Chinese firms trying to go West will face a tough road and the West will miss

Table 8.2   The response: recommendations for China

Political	Companies	Social
• Clarify the roles of various government agencies in business • Systematize and simplify the approval process for Chinese companies to "Go West"	• Partner with experienced local advisors • Invest in international training for executives • Don't rush to invest in overseas expansion • Adopt a proactive approach to corporate communications • Seek to implement global business best practices	• Increase cross-cultural education to bridge the "trust gap" across all parties

opportunities. Bridging the trust gap will not be easy to accomplish, given that geopolitically, China and many Western nations have complex relationships. The more that both sides recognize how they perceive one another, the more likely the mutually beneficial potential of Chinese investment can be maximized (Table 8.2).

Recommendations for the Chinese government

Clarify the role of government agencies in business: perception is reality

Western governments and societies will continue to view Chinese firms with suspicion until there is greater transparency about the role that various Chinese government agencies play in business. Chapter 1 introduced the core characteristics that distinguish Chinese companies from established Western multinational firms. One of the most striking differences is China's state-owned enterprises (SOEs). These SOEs receive tremendous access to capital through state-owned banks, their top leaders are appointed by the state, and they benefit from preferential government policies that in some cases may give them an unfair competitive advantage over private firms. All of these practices occur under a veil of secrecy that leads many in the West to question Chinese government agencies' real motivations and role in the business realm. As the Asia Society notes: "The lack of transparency that shrouds China's leading firms often has to do with protecting the privileged parties who enjoy the resulting profit streams, rather than providing cover for nefarious overseas intentions."[13] Beijing would be wise to prioritize reforming the corporate governance of its firms, especially state-owned enterprises, and improving transparency about the connection between government agencies and business in China.

> The lack of transparency that shrouds China's leading firms often has to do with protecting the privileged parties who enjoy the resulting profit streams, rather than providing cover for nefarious overseas intentions. – *Asia Society*

Systematize and simplify the approval process for Chinese companies to "Go West"

The current system for Chinese companies to expand overseas is overly complex, requiring Chinese firms to coordinate across multiple government bodies and encumbering M&A deal approvals and access to necessary foreign currencies. The EUROCHAM report discussed in Chapter 3 presented results from a survey of 74 Chinese executives who had completed at least one investment in an EU country. Respondents unanimously felt the current approval process is too complicated and urged the Chinese government to provide more straightforward outbound investment procedures. The complexity of the current system makes it difficult for smaller companies with limited resources to navigate, indirectly putting larger or state-owned firms with capital at an advantage. There are various interpretations about how the system works depending on the type of investment, but it is always seen as highly convoluted.

Despite the current byzantine web of government agencies involved in approving overseas investments by Chinese firms, the process is gradually becoming more streamlined. The NDRC instituted new measures in 2012 that allow Chinese firms with overseas subsidiaries to make investments from their subsidiary into other overseas markets without prior approval. The measures also raised the threshold investment amount for NDRC review by ten times. NDRC approval is not necessary for "resources development projects" below $300 million or "non-resources projects" under $100 million.[14] The Chinese government should continue to streamline the approval process for Chinese companies investing in the West, particularly for private firms operating in industries not deemed sensitive.

Recommendations for Chinese companies

Chapter 3 argues that most Chinese companies are not yet ready to "go West." However, the only way they will gain the necessary experience and capabilities to do so is by learning from their own initial mistakes and those made by the Chinese companies that expanded internationally before them. Many of the challenges Chinese companies encounter when expanding into developed Western markets are due to their limited operating experience compared with their Western competitors and the lack of globally experienced leadership at the helm of their companies. The following section lists five recommendations for Chinese companies expanding into Western markets. While there are certainly other recommendations that could be added to this list, implementing these five recommendations will greatly improve a company's likelihood of success.

1: Partner with experienced local advisors

Chinese companies expanding into Germany, France, the US or other developed markets should hire a team of advisors on the ground to help navigate the local business environment. Chinese firms cannot expect Western governments to provide the same level of support and guidance that they receive from the Chinese government back home. An experienced local advisor will be invaluable regardless of investment size, or how straightforward the process may initially seem. It may be more comfortable to communicate in Mandarin with a China-based advisor, but their reputation and experience advising on business in China is unlikely to transfer to doing business in the West. Advisors to consider include locally based lawyers, accountants, public relations firms, and management consultants. Chinese executives do not want to be the next to invest in a wind farm too close to a naval base, and then find their controversial deal making headlines around the world. Find the right partner to get it right the first time.

2: Invest in international training for executives

As internationally experienced 'sea turtles' swim back to China and more globally traveled Chinese managers assume leadership, Chinese companies will adopt a more global approach. However, as Chapter 4 predicts, it will take a generation for the global talent shift to occur. In the meantime, a growing number of Chinese companies are already considering international expansion now. These executives would be wise to enter global training programs such as executive MBAs from Western universities to gain greater exposure to Western business practices, local culture, and languages. This goes for the overseas leadership running international operations as well as senior-level decision-makers back at corporate headquarters in China. As long as Chinese firms remain highly centralized in making business decisions, headquarters leadership needs to understand the overseas environments in which its employees are operating. Even the most globally experienced Chinese executive leading European or North American operations will be ineffective if his or her superiors do not understand the realities of the overseas operating environment. As Chinese companies expand overseas, they should implement a systematic global rotation program to ensure that over time the entire organization becomes more globally minded.

3: Don't rush to invest in overseas expansion

Mergers and acquisitions is becoming the preferred path for Chinese companies entering Western markets for the first time. As Chapter 5 explained, through acquisitions Chinese firms gain access to new markets, increased technological and managerial capabilities, and established global brands. The struggling economic environment in many Western countries means there may be numerous potential acquisition targets for Chinese companies to consider. Chinese firms should be mindful that even though they have significant capital, it may be better to first acquire a minority stake in the overseas target business rather than seek an all-out acquisition.

David Edgerton,[15] a China specialist, discusses a deal he was working on for a large Chinese company. Edgerton introduced the Chinese CEO to the head of a German firm. The German executive wanted $200 million for a 51 percent stake in a project. The Chinese CEO responded: "We have plenty of money. Why don't we just buy the entire project from you instead?" The German executive was looking for a partner, not a buyer. He decided to work with another company as he was put off by the Chinese CEO's seemingly brazen offer.[16] Conversely, CNOOC took the more gradual approach of first taking a minority stake in US-based Chesapeake Energy and then increased its investment after gaining experience working with Chesapeake for multiple years. This was after CNOOC learned from its failed 2005 high-profile bid for Unocal in the US. It is not in Chinese firms' interests to be viewed as "buying up the world." Starting with a low-profile minority position could be the better path to take at first.

4: Adopt a proactive approach to corporate communications

Chinese companies cannot simply focus on growing their business overseas without implementing a cohesive global corporate communications program. Early in its development, Huawei concentrated on expanding overseas, but it did not proactively address media speculation about the close ties between its founder and the People's Liberation Army. After years of repetition in articles and by interest groups, it may be too late for Huawei to shed this image. The firm is playing catch-up now by hiring several multinational public relations, advertising, and marketing agencies. According to Kaiser Kuo, Head of International Communications for Chinese internet giant Baidu: "Chinese companies are tarred with the brush of 'Brand China'. They need to aggressively hire local talent for high-profile positions and give them real decision-making authority. Emphasize the true extent of localization.

Make sure to clearly communicate your brand, value, and mission."[17] These recommendations essentially tell Chinese executives to do everything within their power not to leave things open for adverse interpretation and to take a proactive approach to corporate communications.

> Chinese companies cannot simply focus on growing their business overseas without implementing a cohesive global corporate communications program.

5: Seek to implement global business best practices

As discussed in Chapter 1, Chinese firms differ in how they are structured and how they are run. A state-owned conglomerate in the chemical sector is very different from a private biotechnology company run by a 'sea turtle'. In addition to taking a proactive approach to corporate communications, Chinese companies should seek to implement global business standards. For example, by reforming or improving corporate governance practices, a Chinese company may boost its international image while also identifying new ways to differentiate itself from other domestic firms. One way might be to establish an accredited business council that only grants membership to Chinese companies that meet strict global guidelines for accounting standards or corporate social responsibility practices. While organizations like the China General Chamber of Commerce in the US and China UK Business Association already exist to advance the business interests of Chinese firms overseas, the only criterion their members must meet is that they are Chinese firms operating in the US or UK. An accredited business council could even be administered by a joint China–West advisory board. To be admitted, companies would have to meet strict standards with regard to transparency of ownership structures, corporate social responsibility, financial reporting, etc. By joining this selective business council, Chinese members would signal that they truly are different from other Chinese firms, and at the same time gain third-party recognition through the joint advisory board that their operations meet global business norms (Table 8.3).

Table 8.3 Summary table: recommended responses for the West and China

	Political	Companies	Social
The West	1. Clearly state the areas in which Chinese investment is welcome	1. Ensure fair play among competitors	1. Increase cross-cultural education to bridge the "trust gap" across all parties
	2. Implement an objective framework for threat assessment	2. Consider industry impact when forming partnerships	
	3. Remove politics from investment review to the greatest extent possible	3. Assess the viability of Chinese ownership through M&A	
	4. Systematize and coordinate the promotion of Chinese investment at national and local levels		
China	1. Clarify the roles of various government agencies in business	1. Partner with experienced local advisors	1. Increase cross-cultural education to bridge the "trust gap" across all parties
	2. Systematize and simplify the approval process for Chinese companies to "Go West"	2. Invest in international training for executives	
		3. Don't rush to invest in overseas expansion	
		4. Adopt a proactive approach to corporate communications	
		5. Seek to implement global business best practices	

Conclusion: key takeaways for all parties

Increasing Chinese investment in the West impacts all parties. Adopting the appropriate response is critical to ensuring that all sides benefit from increased Chinese investment, while minimizing any potential concerns. Western governments should adopt a clear and consistent regulatory framework to assess national security and anti-competitive concerns, while better coordinating national and local levels. They should communicate at the most senior level of government that their country welcomes Chinese investment, while clearly articulating which types of investment are prohibited or subject to greater scrutiny. Western governments should implement a clearly defined and communicated process for recruiting and regulating Chinese investment. At the same time, Western companies should carefully evaluate the potential long-term and short-term costs and benefits to competing, partnering, or being acquired by Chinese firms.

The Chinese government must also make efforts to improve how its companies are perceived in the West. At a basic level, it should seek to be more transparent about what "capitalism with Chinese characteristics" actually means. For instance, what is the actual relationship between government agencies and state-owned firms? Without greater clarity about how Chinese government agencies and business are connected in China, Western governments and societies alike will remain skeptical about the underlying motivations of Chinese firms entering their borders. The Chinese government should also continue to streamline the approval process for Chinese companies investing overseas. Chinese firms – and Western economies – may miss out on investment opportunities if they must wait for excessive periods of time while their paperwork moves through the regulatory machine.

Chinese companies face a long list of challenges and obstacles on their path to becoming global firms. They need to understand that partnering with local advisors will help ensure they make the right decisions from the beginning in new markets. Executives running international Chinese firms will benefit from even greater first-hand exposure to foreign cultures and languages in order to understand the business operating conditions in which their overseas teams work. Chinese firms may need to take a more modest approach to foreign direct investment – investing less capital in the short term for a minority position, to build trust and credibility before seeking an all-out acquisition. Chinese firms should adopt a proactive approach to corporate communications in the West to dispel mistaken perceptions about 'Brand China'. Lastly, Chinese firms that seek to implement global standards should identify ways to use this as an opportunity to differentiate themselves from other domestic firms – an accredited Chinese business council could be one possible path.

These concluding recommendations to the governments, companies, and societies of China and the West are focused on improving the current state of Chinese overseas investment. However, for meaningful long-term change to take place, it will take a generation of new leaders from both sides and from government, business, and society to tackle longstanding misperceptions and increase mutual understanding.

***

This book is only the beginning of what is very likely to become an ongoing dialogue across all parties about the rise of Chinese multinational companies in the West. In writing this book, my intention is to provide readers in Chinese and Western societies with a basic understanding of this highly complex and increasingly important phenomenon. It is my hope that many of the bright minds that contributed their perspective to *China Goes West* will build upon this foundational work and write more in-depth accounts of the various topics introduced here. Readers should use the facts and frameworks presented in this book to objectively assess and evaluate the impact the increasing internationalization of Chinese firms will have on their businesses and communities.

China is going West. Its firms will irrevocably reshape the global business landscape. Their investments bring tangible benefits as well as potential concerns. Adopting appropriate measures to address both sides of this growing trend – by all parties – is critical to achieving maximum economic and political benefits.

Notes

Introduction

1. The term "West" is used loosely in this book to describe investment in a range of developed markets including: the United States, European Union, Australia, and Canada. While many of the topics introduced are also applicable to Chinese companies operating in any international market, the primary focus of this book is on "the West" as defined above.

Chapter 1: The Chemical Noodle Firm: What Makes Chinese Companies Different?

1. Koch, Tomas and Oliver Ramsbottom. "A growth strategy for a Chinese state-owned enterprise: An Interview with ChemChina's president." *The McKinsey Quarterly*. July 2008. Web. [http://www.mckinsey.it/storage/first/uploadfile/attach/140408/file/grst08.pdf].
2. China National Blue Star Homepage (Chinese). "China National Blue Star Homepage (Chinese)." 2013. Web. 8 September 2013. [http://www.china-bluestar.com/lanxing/].
3. Koch, Tomas and Oliver Ramsbottom. "Interview with ChemChina's president." *The McKinsey Quarterly*. July 2008. [http://www.mckinsey.it/storage/first/uploadfile/attach/140408/file/grst08.pdf].
4. Malan Noodle Homepage. "Brief Introduction." 2013. Web. 8 September 2013. [http://www.malan.com.cn/modules/tinyd0/index.php?id=2].
5. Colvin, Geoff. "Zhang Ruimin: Management's next icon." *Fortune*. July 2011. Web. [http://management.fortune.cnn.com/2011/07/15/zhang-ruimin-managements-next-icon/].

6. Caijing Guancha. "Guoyouqiye haishi jiti qiye? Haier jituan chanquan xingzhi zhibian." 7 July 2004. Web. [http://gb.cri.cn/7212/2004/12/07/1166@383635.htm].

7. Hu, Yong. "Huyong: 20 nian haier jiaokeshu." *Sohu.com*. 9 June 2009. Web. [http://it.sohu.com/20050609/n240101464.shtml].

8. Wang, Zhen and Gong Li. "Qingdao guoziwei pilu jianguan Haier jituan xijie." *Zhongguo Jingjiwang*. 4 December 2004. Web. 8 September 2013. [http://www.ce.cn/cysc/telecom/home/news/toutiao/200412/04/t2004 1204_2481405.shtml].

9. Based on a personal interview with a Chinese business veteran who wished to remain anonymous.

10. McGregor, Richard. *The Party: The Secret World of China's Communist Rulers*. London: Penguin Books, 2010. 56. Print.

11. McGregor, Richard. *The Party*. London: Penguin Books, 2010. 53. Print.

12. Scissors, Derek. "Chinese State Owned Enterprises and the US Policy on China." *The Heritage Foundation*. 1 March 2012. Web. [http://www.heritage.org/research/testimony/2012/03/chinese-state-owned-enterprises-and-the-us-policy-on-china#_ftn6].

13. Murck, Christian. Personal interview. 18 March 2013.

14. Cary, Eve. "The 'Hidden' Costs of China's Bad Loans." *The Diplomat*. 6 June 2013. Web. [http://thediplomat.com/china-power/the-hidden-costs-of-chinas-bad-loans/].

15. Wang, Jing. "Unirule: SOEs Register Negative Real Profits." *Caixin Online*. 3 March 2011. Web. [http://english.caixin.com/2011-03-03/100231927.html].

16. Shen, Samuel and Michael Flaherty. "Shadow banking bolsters China Inc as Beijing tightens credit." *Reuters*. 8 July 2013. Web. [http://www.reuters.com/article/2013/07/08/us-china-shadow-idUSBRE96712520130708].

17. Luo, Jun. "Regulating China's Shadow Banking System Isn't Easy." *BloombergBusinessweek*. 25 April 2013. Web. [http://www.businessweek.com/articles/2013-04-25/regulating-chinas-shadow-banking-system-isnt-easy].

18. Chen, Shijie. *China Quarterly Market Review*. Singapore: Frontier Strategy Group, 2013. 4. Print.

19. Zhang, Na. "Guohang jiangshe hubei fengongsi gujieshou dongxing hangkong zichan." *Caijing*. 2 April 2009. Web. [http://www.caijing.com.cn/2009-04-02/110131983.html].

20. Shih, Toh Han. "Debt-ridden East Star Airlines suspends operations." *South China Morning Post*. 19 July 2012. Web. [http://www.scmp.com/article/673510/debt-ridden-east-star-airlines-suspends-operations].

21. Cao, Belinda. "Baidu Leads Internet Gains as NQ Mobile Rallies: China Overnight." *Bloomberg*. 28 July 2013. Web. [http://www.bloomberg.com/news/2013-07-28/baidu-leads-internet-gains-as-nq-mobile-rallies-china-overnight.html].

22. Anderlini, Jamil. "China's Premier Li Keqiang targets smaller role for state." *FT.com*. 17 March 2013. Web. [http://www.ft.com/intl/cms/s/0/77c70e1a-8ed0-11e2-be3a-00144feabdc0.html#axzz2eEjm1BPI].

23. SASAC Homepage. "Yangqi minglu." 2013. Web. 8 September 2013. [http://www.sasac.gov.cn/n1180/n1226/n2425/index.html].

24. Qin, Yongfa. "Yangqi dongshihui shidian de jinzhan he xu jiejue de wenti." *Dongshihui*. 2012. Web. [http://www.dongshihui.com.cn/Magazine/ArticleDetail/410].

25. Barboza, David. "Billions in Hidden Riches for Family of Chinese Leader." *The New York Times*. 25 October 2012. Web. [http://www.nytimes.com/2012/10/26/business/global/family-of-wen-jiabao-holds-a-hidden-fortune-in-china.html?pagewanted=all].

26. Renwu Homepage. "Li Yizhong." 2013. Web. 8 September 2013. [http://renwu.hexun.com/figure_3632.shtml].

27. Fannin, Rebecca. "How I did it: Jack Ma, Alibaba.com." *Inc.com*. 1 January 2008. Web. [http://www.inc.com/magazine/20080101/how-i-did-it-jack-ma-alibaba.html].

28. Bodeen, Christopher. "China's Wanda buys luxury yacht maker Sunseeker." *BloombergBusinessweek*. 19 June 2013. Web. [http://www.businessweek.com/ap/2013-06-19/chinas-wanda-buys-luxury-yacht-maker-sunseeker].

29. Sheng, Ellen. "China's Hunan Taizinai in Provisional Liquidation." *The Wall Street Journal*. 14 April 2010. Web. [http://online.wsj.com/article/SB10001424052702304159304575183683927734358.html].

30. BBK Homepage. "Company Profile." 2013. Web. 8 September 2013. [http://www.gdbbk.com/about.asp?id=526].

31. Wolf, David. Personal interview. 22 March 2013.

32. Anderlini, Jamil. "Chinese industry: Ambitions in excess." *The Financial Times*. 16 June 2013. Web. [http://www.ft.com/intl/cms/s/0/4d5528ec-d412-11e2-8639-00144feab7de.html#axzz2exnPj98C].

33. Zhang, Moran. "China's Debt-Laden Steel Industry on the Brink of Bankruptcy." *International Business Times*. 29 August 2013. Web. [http://www.ibtimes.com/chinas-debt-laden-steel-industry-brink-bankruptcy-1401415].

34. Zhu, Ningzhu. "Steelmakers eye non-steel businesses amid profit crunch." *Xinhua*. 11 September 2013. Web. [http://news.xinhuanet.com/english/china/2013-09/11/c_132712542.htm].

35.   NDRC Homepage. "Wei jianjie." 2013. Web. 8 September 2013. [http://www.ndrc.gov.cn/jj/default.htm].

36.   Zhang, James and John V. Grobowski. "New Draft Rules for China Outbound Investments." *Faegrebd.com*. 17 June 2013. Web. [http://www.faegrebd.com/20094].

37.   MOFCOM Homepage. "Zhuyao zhize." 2013. Web. 8 September 2013. [http://www.mofcom.gov.cn/mofcom/zhizi.shtml].

38.   SASAC Homepage. "Shouye." 2013. Web. 8 September 2013. [http://www.sasac.gov.cn/n1180/index.html].

39.   Naughton, Barry. "SASAC and Rising Corporate Power in China." *China Leadership Monitor*, No. 24 Spring. 8. Web. [http://falcon.arts.cornell.edu/am847/pdf/SASAC1.pdf].

40.   SAFE Homepage. "Jiben jineng." 2013. Web. 8 September 2013. [http://www.safe.gov.cn/].

41.   Wei, Lingling and Carolyn Cui. "China Is Seeking U.S. Assets." *The Wall Street Journal*. 20 May 2013. Web. [http://online.wsj.com/article/SB10001424127887324787004578494632401290050.html].

42.   MOF Homepage. "Shouye." 2013. Web. 8 September 2013. [http://www.mof.gov.cn/].

43.   Larum, John, and Jingmin Qian. *A Long March: The Australia-China Investment Relationship*. Rep. Australia China Business Council, October 2012. Web. 8 September 2013. [http://acbc.com.au/deploycontrol/files/upload/news_nat_fdi_report_oct.pdf].

Chapter 2: Fleeing the Great Game: Why Are Chinese Companies Going Global?

1.   Murphy, Melissa. *Issue in Focus: China's "Going Out" Investment Policy*. Rep. Center for Strategic & International Studies, May 2008. Web. 8 September 2013. [http://csis.org/files/publication/080527_freeman_briefing.pdf].

2.   Qianren Jihua. "Renwu Ku." 2013. Web. 8 September 2013. [http://www.1000plan.org/wiki/index.php?doc-view-1048].

3.   Chan, Cathy and Shannon Pettypiece. "Wuxi Will Acquire AppTec Laboratory for $151 million." *Bloomberg*. 4 January 2008. Web. [http://www.bloomberg.com/apps/news?pid=newsarchive&sid=a1_8iRcL5eiw].

4.   WuXi PharmaTech. *Chinese Premier Li Keqiang Visits WuXi PharmaTech's Headquarters in Shanghai*. 1 April 2013. Print.

5. Chiang, Liangi and Nick Edwards. "China gives nod to strategic industries to aid growth." *Reuters*. 30 May 2012. Web. [http://www.reuters.com/article/2012/05/30/us-china-economy-industries-idUSBRE84T0DK20120530].

6. UNCTADSTAT. "China's outward foreign direct investment flows." 2013. Web. 8 September 2013. [http://unctadstat.unctad.org/TableViewer/tableView.aspx].

7. IBM. *Lenovo to Acquire IBM Personal Computing Division*. 7 December 2004. Print.

8. Rosen, Daniel and Thilo Hanemann. *An American Open Door?* Rep. Asia Society, May 2011. Web. 8 September 2013. [http://asiasociety.org/files/pdf/AnAmericanOpenDoor_FINAL.pdf].

9. Thompson, Derek. "Infographic: How China Manipulates Its Currency." *The Atlantic*. 29 March 2011. Web. [http://www.theatlantic.com/business/archive/2011/03/infographic-how-china-manipulates-its-currency/73201/].

10. Kroeber, Arthur. Personal interview. 18 March 2013.

11. Leutert, Wendy. Personal interview. 12 July 2013.

12. Brautigam, Deborah. "Chinese Workers in Africa." Web blog post. *China in Africa: The Real Story*. 2013. Web. 8 September 2013. [http://www.chinaafricarealstory.com/p/chinese-workers-in-africa-anecdotes.html].

13. Unknown. "95 Chinese Companies Make Fortune 500 Global List 2013." *Caijing*. 9 July 2013. Web. [http://english.caijing.com.cn/2013-07-09/113013450.html].

14. Nye, Joseph. "Think Again: Soft Power." *Foreign Policy*. 23 February 2006. Web. [http://www.foreignpolicy.com/articles/2006/02/22/think_again_soft_power].

15. Yuan, Haiying. Personal interview. 26 March 2013.

16. Bhattacharji, Preeti. "Uighurs and China's Xinjiang Region." *Council on Foreign Relations*. 29 May 2012. Web. [http://www.cfr.org/china/uighurs-chinas-xinjiang-region/p16870].

17. Unknown. "Jinfengkeji wugang: gaosu fazhanzong de lengjing sikao." *Tencent Finance*. 19 October 2011. Web. [http://finance.qq.com/a/2011 1019/005298.htm].

18. Chan, Kevin, Michael Wang and David Xu. "Renewables in China: Opportunity or threat?" *McKinsey on Electric Power and Natural Gas*, 1 (2008): 33. Print.

19. Osnos, Evan. "Green Giant." *The New Yorker*. 21 December 2009. Web. [http://www.newyorker.com/reporting/2009/12/21/091221fa_fact_osnos?currentPage=all].

20. Wei, Margaret. Personal interview. 30 March 2013.

21. Unknown. "Ruye san jutou shoufen nianbao gongbu guangming jing lirun jiang 234%." *Sina Finance*. 31 March 2009. Web. [http://finance.sina.com.cn/stock/s/20090331/00116044116.shtml].

22. Bathgate, Adrian. "China's Bright Dairy invests in NZ's Synliat." *Reuters*. 18 July 2010. Web. [http://www.reuters.com/article/2010/07/19/us-bright foods-synlait-idUSTRE66I02320100719].

23. Wolf, David. Personal interview. 22 March 2013.

24. Unknown. "China's stimulus package." *The Economist*. 12 November 2008. Web. [http://www.economist.com/blogs/theworldin2009/2008/11/chinas_stimulus_package].

25. Kuo, Kaiser. Personal interview. 19 March 2013.

26. Li, Fangfang. "Zoomlion speeds up overseas expansion." *China Daily*. 28 September 2012. Web. [http://www.chinadaily.com.cn/china/2012-09/28/content_15790057.htm].

Chapter 3: The Unprepared: Are Chinese Companies Prepared to Go West?

1. Wolf, David. "Should Li-Ning Be Taking On America Now?" Web log post. *Silicon Hutong*. N.p., 21 January 2011. Web. 8 September 2013. [http://siliconhutong.com/2011/01/21/should-li-ning-be-taking-on-america-now].

2. Brettman, Allan. "Jury Awards $1.25 Million to Ex-Li Ning Sports USA Executive." *The Oregonian*. 21 June 2013. Web. [http://www.oregonlive.com/playbooks-profits/index.ssf/2013/06/jury_awards_125_million_to_ex-.html].

3. Shay, Christopher. "Can China's Big Shoe Brand Make Tracks in the US?" *TIME*. 26 March 2010. Web. [http://content.time.com/time/printout/0,8816,1975176,00.html].

4. Calle, Franklyn. "Li-Ning Aiming Global." *Slam Online*. 17 September 2010. Web. [http://www.slamonline.com/online/kicks/2010/09/li-ning-aiming-global/].

5. Brettman, Allan. "Li Ning Portland Operation Shrinks as Chinese Parent's Shares Plunge." *The Oregonian*. 26 May 2011. Web. [http://www.oregonlive.com/business/index.ssf/2011/05/li_ning_portland_operation_shr.html].

6. Lin, Seping. "Wang Qishan de yi piao liangshui." *Sina Finance*. 11 March 2009. Web. [http://finance.sina.com.cn/review/20090311/02055957671.shtml].

7. Doctoroff, Tom. *Billions: Selling to the New Chinese Consumer*. New York: Palgrave Macmillan, 2005. 16. Print.

8. Cucino, Davide, Thomas Rodemer, and Charles-Edouard Bouée. *Chinese Outbound Investment in the European Union*. Rep. Beijing: European Union Chamber of Commerce in China, 2013. Print.

9.   CFIUS Homepage. "The Committee on Foreign Investment in the United States (CFIUS)." 2013. Web. 8 September 2013. [http://www.treasury.gov/resource-center/international/Pages/Committee-on-Foreign-Investment-in-US.aspx].

10. Allen, Craig. Personal interview. 27 March 2013.

11. Ni, Pin. Personal interview. 28 May 2013.

12. Wei, Margaret. Personal interview. 30 March 2013.

13. Thampi, Jai. Personal interview. 1 September 2013.

14. Gillet, Kit. "In China, Executives Flock Back to School for Unfinished Business." *The New York Times.* 27 March 2013. Web. [http://www.nytimes.com/2013/03/27/education/in-china-executives-flock-back-to-graduate-school.html?pagewanted=all].

15. Barton, Dominic and Mei Ye. "Developing China's business leaders: A conversation with Yingyi Qian." July 2013. Web. [http://www.mckinsey.com/insights/leading_in_the_21st_century/developing_chinas_business_leaders].

16. Clearfield, Matthew. Personal interview. 26 August 2013.

17. Crain, Michael. Personal interview. 19 March 2013.

18. Whitaker, Joel. Personal interview. 8 September 2013.

19. Yuan, Haiying. Personal interview. 26 March 2013.

20. Harris, Dan. Personal interview. 21 May 2013.

21. Kao, John. Personal interview. 25 March 2013.

Chapter 4: Global Recognition: Can Chinese Firms Build Global Brands?

1. Jiang, Limei. "Jianlibao ceng maixia niuyuediguodasha yicenglou juzi zhichi lining chuangye." *Xinhua.* 28 April 2013. Web. [http://news.xinhuanet.com/fortune/2013-04/28/c_115576651.htm].

2. Shea, Jack. Personal interview. 20 April 2013.

3. Wolf, David. Personal interview. 22 March 2013.

4. Doctoroff, Tom. Personal interview. 5 March 2013.

5. Webber, Alan M. "What Great Brands Do." *Fast Company.* August 1997. Web. [http://www.fastcompany.com/29056/what-great-brands-do].

6. Schiavenza, Matt. "Why You Haven't Heard of Any Chinese Brands." *The Atlantic.* 8 April 2013. Web. [http://www.theatlantic.com/china/archive/2013/04/why-you-havent-heard-of-any-chinese-brands/274736/].

7. Wolf, David. Personal interview. 22 March 2013.

8. Doctoroff, Tom. Personal interview. 5 March 2013.

9. Knapp, Justin. Personal interview. 4 June 2013.

10. "Simon Sinek on How great leaders inspire action." www.ted.com. Web. 4 May 2010. [http://www.ted.com/talks/simon_sinek_how_great_leaders_inspire_action.html].

11. Black, Bill. Personal interview. 29 January 2013.

12. Markman, Scott. Personal interview. 24 May 2013.

13. Doctoroff, Tom. Personal interview. 5 March 2013.

14. Booty, Ed. Personal interview. 4 April 2013.

15. Unknown. "Pearl River Piano: Building a Chinese Brand for the Global Market." *CKGSB Knowledge.* 28 April 2010. Web. [http://knowledge.ckgsb.edu.cn/2010/08/28/china-business-strategy/pearl-river-piano-building-a-chinese-brand-for-the-global-market/].

16. Xiang, Bing. "Zhujiang gangqin: cong bentu zhizao zhuanxiang quanqiu yunying." *Sina Finance.* 28 June 2011. Web. [http://finance.sina.com.cn/emba/ckgsb/20110628/154610060487.shtml].

17. O'Connell, Patricia. "TCL Multimedia's Global Agenda." *Bloomberg Businessweek.* 21 August 2005. Web. [http://www.businessweek.com/stories/2005-08-21/online-extra-tcl-multimedias-global-agenda].

18. Cook, Nancy. Personal interview. 9 September 2013.

19. Gluckman, Ron. "Appliances for Everyone." *Forbes.* 25 April 2012. Web. [http://www.forbes.com/global/2012/0507/global-2000-12-feature-haier-zhang-ruimin-appliances.html].

20. Kauffmann, Sylvie. "Looking for McDonalds in China: Can Emerging Economies Build Global Brands?" *Le Monde/World Crunch.* 13 September 2012. Web. [http://www.worldcrunch.com/business-finance/looking-for-mcdonald-039-s-in-china-can-emerging-economies-build-global-brands-/samsung-iphone-apple-economy-smartphone/c2s9522/].

21. Rein, Shaun. *The End of Cheap China.* Hoboken: John Wiley & Sons, 2012. 7. Print.

22. Zhu, Julia Q. Personal interview. 20 February 2013.

23. Roman, David. "Chinese Global Brands? Not Yet." *Forbes.* 8 August 2012. Web. [http://www.forbes.com/sites/china/2012/08/08/chinese-global-brands-not-yet/2/].

Chapter 5: China's Overseas M&A Moment: Buying Up the World's Corporations?

1. Wang, Yuanzhi. "Lishufu: jili binggou woerwo shi fanghuguishanshi shougou." *iCEO.com.* 23 December 2011. Web. [http://www.iceo.com.cn/renwu/35/2011/1223/237826.shtml].

2. Russo, Bill. Personal interview. 28 June 2012.

3. Jiang, Shixue. "How to get the eggs into the right basket." *China Daily USA*. 26 October 2012. Web. [http://usa.chinadaily.com.cn/business/2012-10/26/content_15850467_2.htm].

4. Lee, Melanie. "China vehicles to top 200 million in 2020 – report." *Reuters*. 5 September 2010. Web. [http://www.reuters.com/article/2010/09/06/autos-china-idUSTOE68401I20100906].

5. Waldmeir, Patti. "Geely grapples with Volvo gears." *Financial Times*. 23 April 2013. Web. [http://www.ft.com/intl/cms/s/0/bdb705c6-abcf-11e2-8c63-00144feabdc0.html#axzz2cVWQd599].

6. Williamson, Peter. Personal interview. 1 June 2012.

7. Beddor, Christopher. "Stepping Out: The Globalization Strategies of Chinese Companies." *CKGSB Knowledge*. 22 February 2013. Web. [http://knowledge.ckgsb.edu.cn/2013/02/22/globalization/stepping-out-the-globalization-strategies-of-chinese-companies/].

8. Shen, Hong. "Sany, Citic Buy Germany's Putzmeister." *The Wall Street Journal*. 30 January 2012. Web. [http://online.wsj.com/article/SB10001424052970204652904577192601606351164.html].

9. Burkitt, Laurie. "Chinese Food Company Eats English Breakfast." *The Wall Street Journal*. 3 May 2012. Web. [http://online.wsj.com/article/SB10001424052702304746604577381292023843930.html].

10. Mider, Zachary R. "China's Wanda to Buy AMC Cinema Chain for $2.6 Billion." *Bloomberg*. 21 May 2012. Web. [http://www.bloomberg.com/news/2012-05-21/china-s-wanda-group-to-buy-amc-cinema-chain-for-2-6-billion.html].

11. Leggett, Richard. Personal interview. 8 September 2013.

12. Pettis, Michael. Personal interview. 19 March 2013.

13. Ulrich, Jing. "Upwards and Onwards: China's Outbound M&A." *J.P. Morgan's Hands-On China*. 21 January 2013. Web. [https://markets.jpmorgan.com/research/EmailPubServlet?action=open&hashcode=u31ot16h&doc=GPS-1031340-0].

14. Perkowski, Jack. Personal interview. 30 March 2013.

15. Perkowski, Jack. Personal interview. 30 March 2013.

16. McGregor, James. *One Billion Customers*. New York: Free Press, 2005. 58. Print.

17. Kirchfeld, Aaron. "China Goes Shopping for German Factories." *BloombergBusinessweek*. 14 June 2012. Web. [http://www.businessweek.com/articles/2012-06-14/china-goes-shopping-for-german-factories].

18. Nash, Tony. Personal interview. 6 August 2012.

19. Kwong, Ray. "China on Track to Be World's Largest Luxury E-Commerce Market by 2015." *Forbes*. 31 May 2012. Web. [http://www.forbes.com/

sites/raykwong/2012/05/31/china-on-track-to-be-worlds-largest-luxury-e-commerce-market-by-2015/].

20. Export.gov Homepage. "Doing Business in China – Marine Industries." Web. 11 September 2013. [http://export.gov/china/doingbizinchina/eg_cn_025861.asp].

21. Unknown. "Chinese group purchases controlling interest in Ferretti." BoatingIndustry.com. 10 January 2012. Web. [http://www.boatingindustry.com/news/2012/01/10/chinese-group-purchases-controlling-interest-in-ferretti/].

22. Chan, Jenny. "China's brands head west." Campaign Magazine. April 2012: 44–47. Print.

23. Burkitt, Laurie. "Chinese Food Company Eats English Breakfast." The Wall Street Journal. 3 May 2012. Web. [http://online.wsj.com/article/SB1000142405270230474660457738129202384393.html].

24. Yang, Hao. "Guangmingshipin wangzongnan chuhai xinjing." 21cbr.com. 29 May 2012. Web. [http://www.21cbr.com/html/magzine/2012/97/hot/2012/0529/9591.html].

25. Thomas, Denny. "China Bright Food to buy Manassen for over $516 million." Reuters. 14 August 2011. Web. [http://www.reuters.com/article/2011/08/14/us-brightfood-manassen-idUSTRE77D19C20110814].

26. Guo, Aibing and Jeremy van Loon. "Cnooc Buys Nexen in China's Top Overseas Acquisition." Bloomberg. 23 July 2012. Web. [http://www.bloomberg.com/news/2012-07-23/cnooc-to-buy-canada-s-nexen-for-15-1-billion-to-expand-overseas.html].

Chapter 6: The Concerns: Should the West Worry about Chinese Investment?

1. Huawei.com Homepage. "Financial Highlights." Web. 11 September 2013. [http://www.huawei.com/en/about-huawei/corporate-info/financial/index.htm].

2. ZTE Corporation. 2012 Annual Report. Shenzhen, China. Highlights of accounting and financial indicators. 14 September 2013 [http://wwwen.zte.com.cn/en/about/investor_relations/corporate_report/annual_report/201304/P020130414667427851218.pdf].

3. Salant, Jonathan D. and Kathleen Miller. "ZTE Quadruples Lobbying After U.S. House Blacklisting." Bloomberg. 30 August 2013. Web. [http://www.

bloomberg.com/news/2013-08-30/zte-quadruples-lobbying-after-u-s-house-blacklisting.html].

4. Huawei. *Huawei CEO & Founder Gives First Ever Interview on Global Corporate Outlook*. 12 May 2013. Print.

5. Official Hearing Recording. *Huawei and ZTE Testify Before House Intel Committee Part 1*. Posted by RepMikeRogers.13 September 2012. Web. [http://www.youtube.com/watch?v=ApQjSCUpt4s].

6. Official Hearing Recording. Posted by RepMikeRogers. 13 September 2012.

7. Official Hearing Recording. Posted by RepMikeRogers. 13 September 2012.

8. Rogers, Mike and Dutch Ruppersberger. *Investigative Report on the U.S. National Security Issues Posed by Chinese Telecommunications Companies Huawei and ZTE*. 8 October 2012. Print.

9. Anderson, Eric C. Personal interview. 1 March 2013.

10. Goldkorn, Jeremy. "Transformers and Wikipedia." *Danwei.org*. 21 August 2007. Web. [http://www.danwei.org/media_regulation/transfomers_and_wikipedia_open.php].

11. Wagnleitner, Reinhold., trans. Wolf, Diane M. Coca-Colonization and the Cold War. Chapel Hill, North Carolina: The University of North Carolina Press: 1994.

12. Unknown. "Friendly locusts." *The Economist*. 23 February 2006. Web. [http://www.economist.com/node/5557472].

13. Meunier, Sophie. *A Faustian Bargain or Just a Good Bargain? Chinese Foreign Direct Investment and Politics in Europe*. Princeton, New Jersey: Princeton University. 2013. Print.

14. Younglai, Rachelle. "Obama blocks Chinese wind farms in Oregon over security." *Reuters*. 29 September 2012. Web. [http://www.reuters.com/article/2012/09/29/us-usa-china-turbines-idUSBRE88R19220120929].

15. Barboza, David. "China backs away from Unocal bid." *The New York Times*. 3 August 2005. Web. [http://www.nytimes.com/2005/08/02/business/worldbusiness/02iht-unocal.html?_r=0].

16. Carew, Sinead and Jessica Wohl. "Huawei backs away from 3Leaf acquisition." *Reuters*. 19 February 2011. Web. [http://www.reuters.com/article/2011/02/19/us-huawei-3leaf-idUSTRE71I38920110219].

17. Jackson, James K. "The Committee on Foreign Investment in the United States (CFIUS)." *Congressional Research Service*. 12 June 2013. Web. [http://www.fas.org/sgp/crs/natsec/RL33388.pdf].

18. Congresswoman Rosa DeLauro. *DeLauro Calls for Comprehensive Review of Shuanghui International Holdings-Smithfield Foods Deal*. 17 July 2013. Web. [http://delauro.house.gov/index.php?option=com_content&view=article&id=1344:delauro-calls-for-comprehensive-review-of-

shuanghui-international-holdings-smithfield-foods-deal&catid=2:2012-press-releases&Itemid=21].

19. Hanemann, Thilo and Beibei Bao. "A New Momentum for FDI Reform in China." *Rhodium Group.* 28 August 2013. Web. [http://rhg.com/notes/a-new-momentum-for-fdi-reforms-in-china].

20. Sauvant, Karl P. and Huiping Chen. "A China – US Bilateral Investment Treaty." *Colombia FDI Perspectives.* 27 December 2012. Web. [http://www.vcc.columbia.edu/content/china-us-bilateral-investment-treaty-template-multilateral-framework-investment].

21. Shalal-Esa, Andrea. "Pentagon insists it is open to foreign investment in the U.S." *Reuters.* 31 August 2013. Web. [http://www.reuters.com/article/2013/08/31/us-usa-military-foreign-idUSBRE97U03G20130831].

22. U.S. Deparement of Treasury. *Committee on Foreign Investment in the United States – Annual Report.* December 2012. Print.

23. Kroeber, Arthur. Personal interview. 18 March 2013.

24. Nicholson, Chris V. "Cnooc in $2.2 Billion Deal with Chesapeake Energy." *The New York Times.* 11 October 2010. Web. [http://dealbook.nytimes.com/2010/10/11/cnooc-in-2-2-billion-deal-with-chesapeake-energy/].

25. Hook, Leslie and Bernard Simon. "Cnooc to acquire Opti Canada for $2.1bn." *The Financial Times.* 20 July 2011. Web. [http://www.ft.com/intl/cms/s/0/164c9e2c-b2d9-11e0-bc28-00144feabdc0.html#axzz2effcx1my].

26. Guo, Aibing and Jeremy van Loon. "Cnooc Buys Nexen in China's Top Overseas Acquisition." *Bloomberg.* 23 July 2012. Web. [http://www.bloomberg.com/news/2012-07-23/cnooc-to-buy-canada-s-nexen-for-15-1-billion-to-expand-overseas.html].

27. Fuller, Thomas. "French fear eye of 'ogre' is on Danone." *The New York Times.* 21 July 2005. Web. [http://www.nytimes.com/2005/07/20/business/worldbusiness/20iht-danone.html?_r=0].

28. Stynes, Tess. "General Mills Goes for Yoplait." *The Wall Street Journal.* 19 May 2011. Web. [http://online.wsj.com/article/SB1000142405274870342120457633114 4068424456.html].

29. Meunier, Sophie. Personal interview. 20 June 2013.

30. WTO.org Homepage. "Find disputes cases." Web. 12 September 2013. [http://www.wto.org/english/tratop_e/dispu_e/find_dispu_cases_e.htm#results].

31. Yap, Chuin-Wei. "Sinovel Wind to Shut Four Overseas Subsidiaries." *The Wall Street Journal.* 3 July 2013. Web. [http://online.wsj.com/article/SB100014241278873244361045785811104 94296552.html].

32. Blair, Dennis C. and Jon M. Huntsman Jr. *The IP Commission Report*. May 2013. Print.

33. Unknown. "Greek president hails COSCO's Piraeus project." *China Daily*. 31 May 2013. Web. [http://www.chinadaily.com.cn/china/2013-05/31/content_16549514.htm].

34. Alderman, Liz. "Under Chinese, a Greek Port Thrives." *The New York Times*. 11 October 2012. Web. [http://www.nytimes.com/2012/10/11/business/global/chinese-company-sets-new-rhythm-in-port-of-piraeus.html?pagewanted=all&gwh=EF7317A3C65D20CAA88899153D8E6AC9].

35. Meunier, Sophie. Personal interview. 20 June 2013.

36. Lim, Louisa. "In Greek Port, Storm Brews Over Chinese-Run Labor." *The New York Times*. 8 June 2011. Web. [http://www.npr.org/2011/06/08/137035251/in-greek-port-storm-brews-over-chinese-run-labor].

Chapter 7: The Opportunity: How Can the West Benefit from Chinese Investment?

1. White, Joseph B and Norihiko Shirouzu. "In the Heart of the Rust Belt, Chinese Funds Provide the Grease." *The Wall Street Journal*. 11 February 2012. Web. [http://online.wsj.com/article/SB10001424052970203735304577163741272699930.html].

2. Remenar, Robert. Personal interview. 29 April 2013.

3. World Economic Forum. *Emerging Best Practices of Chinese Globalizers*. 2012. Print.

4. Jiang, Shixue. "How to get the eggs into the right basket." *China Daily USA*. 26 October 2012. Web. [http://usa.chinadaily.com.cn/business/2012-10/26/content_15850467_2.htm].

5. Jiang, Shixue. "Chinese investment in the EU: a win-win game." *European Policy Centre*. 25 February 2013. Web. [http://www.epc.eu/pub_details.php?cat_id=4&pub_id=3344&year=2013].

6. Hanemann, Thilo. "The employment impacts of Chinese investment in the United States." *East Asia Forum*. 30 October 2012. Web. [http://www.eastasiaforum.org/2012/10/30/the-employment-impacts-of-chinese-investment-in-the-united-states/].

7. American Society of Civil Engineers. *2013 Report Card for America's Infrastructure*. 2013. Web.

8. Schwartz, John. "Obama Fleshes Our Plans for Infrastructure Projects." *The New York Times*. 20 February 2013. Web. [http://www.nytimes.

com/2013/02/20/us/politics/obama-to-flesh-out-plans-for-infrastructure-projects.html].

9. Halper, Daniel. "Kerry Welcomes Chinese Investment in America's Infrastructure." *The Weekly Standard*. 14 April 2013. Web. [http://www.weeklystandard.com/blogs/kerry-welcomes-chinese-investment-americas-infrastructure_716360.html].

10. Zhang, Yuwei. "COSCO forms strong anchor for Boston port." *China Daily USA*. 6 March 2012. Web. [http://usa.chinadaily.com.cn/business/2012-03/06/content_14764208.htm].

11. Deutsche Welle. *Made in Germany|Welcome to Germany – Chinese Investors*. 17 August 2008. Web. [http://www.youtube.com/watch?v=Szs--QWhbTg].

12. Zhang, Danhong. "Chinese firm stands on shoulders of German giant." *DW.de*. 24 March 2010. Web. [http://www.dw.de/chinese-firm-stands-on-shoulders-of-german-giant/a-5385339].

13. Perkowski, Jack. Personal interview. 30 March 2013.

14. Sirkin, Harold L., Michael Zinser and Douglas Hohner. "Made in America, Again." *The Boston Consulting Group*. August 2011. Web. [http://www.bcg.com/documents/file84471.pdf].

15. Ling, John. Personal interview. 15 June 2013.

16. *Foreign Investment in South Carolina: Highlighting China*. South Carolina Department of Commerce. March 2013. Web. [http://sccommerce.com/sites/default/files/document_directory/foreign_china_march_2013.pdf].

17. Sany America. *SANY America Opens Corporate Headquarters in Peachtree City, Georgia*. 30 August 2011. Print.

18. Tomberlin, Michael. "Golden Dragon chooses Alabama's Wilcox County for $100 million copper tubing plant." *Al.com*. 7 February 2012. Web. [http://blog.al.com/businessnews/2012/02/golden_dragon_chooses_alabamas.html].

19. Manzoni, Mike. "Gregory Pipe Mill to Create Hundreds of Jobs." *KRISTV.com*. 2 January 2013. Web. [http://www.kristv.com/news/gregory-pipe-mill-to-create-hundreds-of-jobs/#!prettyPhoto/0/].

20. Sirkin, Harold L., Michael Zinser and Douglas Hohner. "Made in America, Again." *The Boston Consulting Group*. August 2011. Web. [http://www.bcg.com/documents/file84471.pdf].

21. Schmitt, Patrick. "China's Largest Local Brand Goes Global."*thedrinksbusiness.com*. 22 February 2013. Web. [http://www.thedrinksbusiness.com/2013/02/chinas-largest-local-brand-goes-global/].

22. Bradsher, Keith. "China Aims at Europe's Wines After Solar Panel Action." *The New York Times.* 5 June 2013. Web. [http://www.nytimes.com/2013/06/06/business/global/china-to-investigate-eu-wine-after-subsidy-and-dumping-complaints.html?pagewanted=all&_r=0].

23. World Economic Forum. *Emerging Best Practices of Chinese Globalizers.* 2012. Print.

24. Wong, Anson. "Sustainability and Inclusiveness Primer: CSR Guidelines for Chinese Companies Going Global." *CKGSB Knowledge.* 18 July 2013. Web. [http://knowledge.ckgsb.edu.cn/2013/07/18/csr/csr-guidelines-for-chinese-companies-going-global/].

25. United Nations Global Compact Homepage. "Overview of the UN Global Compact." 2013. Web. 13 September 2013. [http://www.unglobalcompact.org/AboutTheGC/index.html].

26. World Economic Forum. *Emerging Best Practices of Chinese Globalizers.* 2012. Print.

27. Flannery, Russell. "China's Wanda Group Donates Tickets, Snacks to U.S. High Schools After AMC Purchase." *Forbes.* 7 September 2012. Web. [http://www.forbes.com/sites/russellflannery/2012/09/07/chinas-wanda-group-donates-tickets-snacks-to-u-s-high-schools-after-amc-purchase/].

28. Goldwind. *Goldwind Signs Donation Agreement with Germany's Saarland University.* 13 July 2012. Print.

29. Kundnani, Hans. "Good and bad interdependence." *European Council on Foreign Relations.* 25 June 2013. Web. [http://ecfr.eu/blog/entry/good_and_bad_interdependence].

Chapter 8: The Response: Maximizing Benefits, Minimizing Concerns

1. Rosen, Daniel and Thilo Hanemann. *An American Open Door?.* Rep. Asia Society, May 2011. Web. 8 September 2013. [http://asiasociety.org/files/pdf/AnAmericanOpenDoor_FINAL.pdf].

2. Kroeber, Arthur. Personal interview. 18 March 2013.

3. Moran, Theodore H. *Foreign Acquisitions and National Security.* Global Forum on International Investment, December 2009. Web. 8 September 2013. [http://www.oecd.org/investment/globalforum/44231376.pdf].

4. Moran, Theodore H. *Foreign Acquisitions and National Security.* Global Forum on International Investment, Dec. 2009. Web. 8 September 2013. [http://www.oecd.org/investment/globalforum/44231376.pdf].

5. Baertlein, Lisa, P.J. Huffstutter and Aditi Shrivastava. "U.S. clears Smithfield's acquisition by China's Shuanghui." *Reuters*. 7 September 2013. Web. [http://www.reuters.com/article/2013/09/07/us-usa-china-smithfield-idUSBRE98513I20130907].

6. Scissors, Derek. "China's Global Investment Rises: The U.S. Should Focus on Competition." *The Heritage Foundation*. 8 January 2013. Web. [http://thf_media.s3.amazonaws.com/2013/pdf/bg2757.pdf].

7. Brickman, Aaron. Personal interview. 29 May 2013.

8. Knapp, Justin. "Michigan Governor Synder's Upcoming Trip to China." *Goodall Focus*. 26 April 2013. Web. [http://goodallfocus.com/2013/04/26/michigan-governor-snyders-upcoming-trip-to-china/].

9. Meunier, Sophie. Personal interview. 20 June 2013.

10. Meunier, Sophie. Personal interview. 20 June 2013.

11. Meunier, Sophie. *A Faustian Bargain or Just a Good Bargain? Chinese Foreign Direct Investment and Politics in Europe*. Princeton, New Jersey: Princeton University. 2013. Print.

12. Wolf, David. Personal interview. 22 March 2013.

13. Rosen, Daniel and Thilo Hanemann. *An American Open Door?*. Rep. Asia Society, May 2011. Web.8 September 2013. [http://asiasociety.org/files/pdf/AnAmericanOpenDoor_FINAL.pdf].

14. Zhang, James and John V. Grobowski. "New Draft Rules for China Outbound Investments." *Faegrebd.com*. 17 June 2013. Web. [http://www.faegrebd.com/20094].

15. Based on a personal interview with a Chinese business specialist who wished to remain anonymous.

16. Based on a personal interview with a Chinese business specialist who wished to remain anonymous.

17. Kuo, Kaiser. Personal interview. 19 March 2013.

Index